# NCS 기반 Business Correspondence Ⅱ

활용편

# PREFACE 머리말

한치 앞도 내다볼 수 없는 무한경쟁, 인공지능의 시대에서도 뛰어난 국제사무인력에 대한 기업의 수요는 더욱 늘어나고 있다. 특히 비서직과 일반 사무직의 주요 업무인 상황에 맞는 적절하고 신속한 커뮤니케이션의 중요성은 아무리 강조해도 지나치지 않다.

〈Business Correspondence 활용편〉은 다양한 영문서 작성의 이론과 실제를 다양한 예문 및 예제를 통해 익히는 데 목적을 두었다. 특히 본 개정판은 국가직무능력표준(NCS, National Competency Standards) 기반으로 구성된 학습자 중심의 실용적 교육서이다.

영문서지원업무의 능력단위요소인 '수신 영문서 내용 파악하기', '영문서 작성 업무 지원하기', '비즈니스 영문서 작성하기'에서 필요한 지식, 기술, 태도를 고루 다루고 있으며, 특히 교수자와 학습자가 서로 상호작용하기 용이하도록 많은 예제를 포함하고 있다.

이 책은 모두 7장으로 이루어져 있다.

Unit1 Requesting & Confirming Service(서비스 요청 및 확인편지)
Unit2 Ordering & Acknowledging Orders(상품 주문 및 접수편지)
Unit3 Claim Letters & Adjustment Letters(배상요청 및 중재편지)
Unit4 Collection Letters & Reply(수금편지와 회신)
Unit5 Follow-up Letters & Congratulations Messages(사후편지 및 축하메시지)
Unit6 Job-related Documents(구직 관련 문서들)
Unit7 Organization-related Terms and Documents(기업 조직 관련 용어와 문서들)

본서가 비즈니스 현장에서 일하는 직장인과 취업을 준비하는 학생들에게 많은 도움이 되길 바란다.

끝으로 이 책이 나오기 까지 애써주신 한올출판사의 여러분들께 감사드린다.

2016. 8.

저자 씀

# CONTENTS 차례

CONTENTS

본서의 개정판은 비서직과 일반 사무직을 위한 영문서 작성의 활용편으로 교수자와 학습자가 서로 상호작용하기 용이하도록 많은 예제를 포함하고 있으며, NCS를 기반으로 개정된 학습자 중심의 실용적 교육서이다.

국가직무능력표준(NCS, National Competency Standards)은 산업현장에서 직무를 행하기 위해 요구되는 지식·기술·태도 등의 내용을 국가가 체계화한 것이다. 직무 유형(Type)을 중심으로 국가직무능력표준의 단계적 구성을 나타낸 분류체계에 따르면 본서의 교과목이 되는 영문서 작성은 아래와 같다.

분류체계 : 02.경영·회계·사무 | 02.총무·인사 | 03.일반사무 | 조회 | 엑셀받기

| 분류체계 | | | | 개발연도 | |
|---|---|---|---|---|---|
| 대분류 | 중분류 | 소분류 | 세분류(직무) | NCS | 학습모듈 |
| 02. 경영·회계·사무 | 02. 총무·인사 | 03. 일반사무 | 01. 비서 | 2013 | |
| | | | 02. 사무행정 | 2013 | |

NCS는 아래의 표와 같이 분류체계의 하위단위로서 능력단위를 기본으로 하여 구성된다.

- 직무는 국가직무능력표준 분류체계의 세분류를 의미하고, 원칙상 세분류 단위에서 표준이 개발 됩니다.
- 능력단위는 국가직무능력표준 분류체계의 하위단위로서 국가직무능력표준의 기본 구성요소에 해당 됩니다.

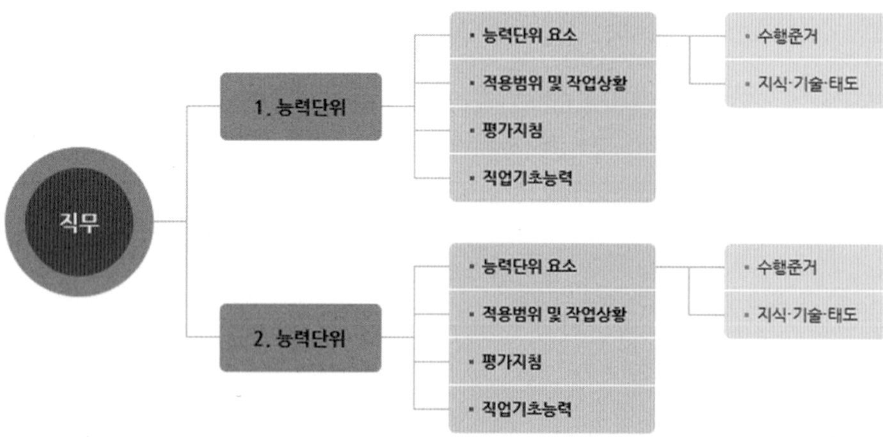


[국가직무능력표준 능력단위 구성]

- 능력단위는 능력단위분류번호, 능력단위정의, 능력단위요소(수행준거, 지식·기술·태도), 적용범위 및 작업상황, 평가지침, 직업기초능력으로 구성

이어서 소개될 능력단위 요소에 대한 수행 준거와 평가 지침은 교수자들에게 본서를 더욱 효과적으로 활용하는데 도움을 줄 것이다.

| | |
|---|---|
| 분류번호 : | |
| 능력단위 명칭 : | 영문서 지원업무 |
| 능력단위 정의 : | 영문서 지원업무는 영어 · 외국어 능력을 통하여 문서관련 업무를 지원하는 능력이다. |

| 능력단위요소 | 수행준거 |
|---|---|
| 수신 영문서 내용 파악하기 | 1.1 영문 비즈니스 관련 용어를 수신 영문서 내용 파악에 활용할 수 있다.<br>1.2 수신된 문서의 종류에 따라 수 · 발신자를 파악할 수 있다.<br>1.3 수신된 문서의 내용을 파악하여 관련자에게 보고할 수 있다. |
| | 【지 식】<br>● 영문서 종류별 구성요소와 형식<br>● 영문법<br>● 영문 비즈니스 용어<br>● 영문 첨삭법 |
| | 【기 술】<br>● 영문작문능력<br>● 영어독해능력<br>● 영문타자능력<br>● 영문서 작성 능력 |
| | 【태 도】<br>● 정확한 문서 작성을 위한 집중력<br>● 문서를 구분할 수 있는 분석적 태도<br>● 적극적인 수용 자세 |
| 영문서 작성 업무 지원하기 | 2.1 영문서 내용에 적합한 영문서 서식을 적용할 수 있다.<br>2.2 상사가 필요로 하는 자료를 수집하여 제공할 수 있다.<br>2.3 상사가 작성한 영문서의 초안을 서식에 맞추어 문서화할 수 있다 |
| | 【지 식】<br>● 영문서 종류별 구성요소와 형식<br>● 영문법<br>● 영문 비즈니스 용어<br>● 영문 첨삭법<br>● 영문 구두점 사용법 |

<table>
<tr><th>능력단위요소</th><th>수행준거</th></tr>
<tr><td rowspan="2">영문서 작성<br>업무 지원하기</td><td>【기 술】<br>● 영문작문능력<br>● 영어독해능력<br>● 영문타자능력<br>● 영문서 작성 능력</td></tr>
<tr><td>【태 도】<br>● 정확한 문서 작성을 위한 집중력<br>● 문서를 구분할 수 있는 분석적 태도<br>● 적극적인 수용 자세</td></tr>
<tr><td rowspan="4">비즈니스 영문서<br>작성하기</td><td>3.1 사용목적에 따른 영문서의 종류에 따라 필요한 구성요소와 형식을 파악할 수 있다.<br>3.2 상사의 지시에 따라 정해진 시간 내에 문법과 형식에 맞추어 영문서를 작성할 수 있다.<br>3.3 정확한 영문서 작성을 위해 초안을 검토하고 상사의 지시에 따라 수정 · 보완할 수 있다.</td></tr>
<tr><td>【지 식】<br>● 영문서 종류별 구성요소와 형식<br>● 영문법<br>● 영문 비즈니스 용어<br>● 영문 첨삭법<br>● 영문 구두점 사용법</td></tr>
<tr><td>【기 술】<br>● 영문작문능력<br>● 영어독해능력<br>● 영문타자능력<br>● 영문서 작성 능력</td></tr>
<tr><td>【태 도】<br>● 정확한 문서 작성을 위한 집중력<br>● 문서를 구분할 수 있는 분석적 태도<br>● 적극적인 수용 자세</td></tr>
</table>

## ⊙ 적용범위 및 작업상황

### 고려사항

- 외국어는 일반적으로 가장 널리 통용되는 영어를 기준으로 작성되었으나, 해당 기관의 환경과 필요에 따라 그 외 외국어(중국어, 일본어 등)로 대체할 수 있다.
- 영문서의 종류는 비즈니스 레터, 이메일, 메모, 팩스, 초청장, 이력서, 커버레터, 송장, 명함, 업무 관련 매뉴얼 등을 포함한다.
- 능력단위요소 '수신 영문서 내용 파악하기'는 수신된 문서의 내용과 목적을 파악하여 정확하게 처리하는 업무를 의미한다.
- 능력단위요소 '영문서 작성 업무 지원하기'는 상사가 작성한 영문서의 내용을 파악하여, 영문서 서식에 맞추어 문서화하는 업무를 의미한다.
- 능력단위요소 '비즈니스 영문서 작성하기'는 비서가 상사의 지시에 따라 문서의 목적을 파악하여 내용을 직접 작성하는 업무를 의미한다.

### 자료 및 관련 서류

- 외국어 사전
- 한국어 사전
- 각종 영문서 서식(비즈니스 레터, 이메일, 메모, 팩스, 초청장, 이력서, 커버레터, 송장, 명함, 업무 관련 매뉴얼)
- 회사소개 안내자료
- 한국 소개자료
- 영문 회사 조직도

### 장비 및 도구

- 컴퓨터
- 프린터
- 복사기
- 문서작성도구
- 사무용 소프트웨어

### 재료

- 해당 없음

## ◉ 평가지침

### 평가방법

- 평가자는 능력단위 국제 업무지원의 수행준거에 제시되어 있는 내용을 평가하기 위해 이론과 실기를 나누어 평가하거나 종합적인 결과물의 평가 등 다양한 평가 방법을 사용할 수 있다.
- 피 평가자의 과정평가 및 결과평가 방법

| 평가방법 | 평가유형 | |
|---|---|---|
| | 과정평가 | 결과평가 |
| A. 포트폴리오 | V | |
| B. 문제해결 시나리오 | | |
| C. 서술형시험 | | V |
| D. 논술형시험 | | |
| E. 사례연구 | | V |
| F. 평가자 질문 | | |
| G. 평가자 체크리스트 | | |
| H. 피평가자 체크리스트 | | |
| I. 일지/저널 | | |
| J. 역할연기 | | |
| K. 구두발표 | | |
| L. 작업장평가 | | |
| M. 기타 | | V |

### 평가항목

- 수행준거에 제시되어 있는 내용을 성공적으로 수행할 수 있는지를 평가해야 한다.
- 평가자는 다음 사항을 평가해야 한다.
  - 영문서 작성능력
  - 문장구조이해능력
  - 상황별 외국어 구사능력

## ⊙ 직업기초능력

| 순 번 | 직 업 기 초 능 력 | |
|---|---|---|
| | 주 요 영 역 | 하 위 영 역 |
| 1 | 의사소통능력 | 문서이해능력, 문서작성능력, 경청능력, 의사표현능력, 기초외국어능력 |
| 2 | 문제해결능력 | 사고력, 문제 처리 능력, |
| 3 | 자기개발능력 | 자아인식능력, 자기관리능력, 경력개발능력 |
| 4 | 자원관리능력 | 시간자원관리능력, 물적자원관리능력 |
| 5 | 대인관계능력 | 팀웍능력, 리더십능력, 갈등관리능력, 협상능력, 고객서비스능력 |
| 6 | 정보관리능력 | 컴퓨터활용능력, 정보처리능력 |
| 7 | 조직이해능력 | 국제감각, 조직체제이해능력, 경영이해능력, 업무이해능력 |
| 8 | 직업윤리 | 근로윤리, 공동체 윤리 |

UNIT 01

# Requesting & Confirming a Service

(서비스 요청 및 확인편지)

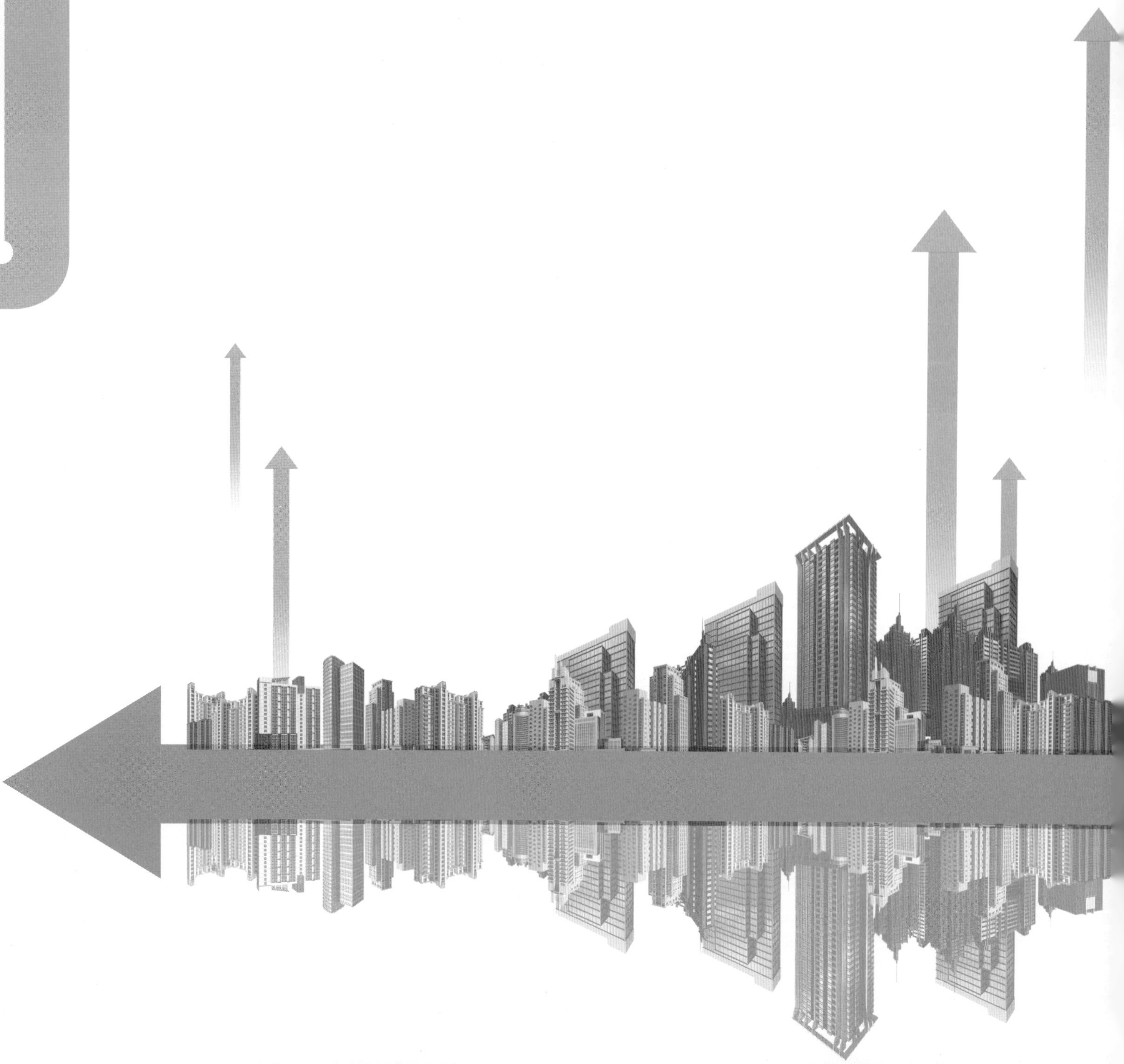

UNIT 01

# Requesting & Confirming a Service
(서비스 요청 및 확인편지)

## 어휘 학습

| | |
|---|---|
| conference | n. 회의 |
| confirm | v. 확인하다 |
| attend | v. 출석하다, 참석하다 |
| additional | a. 부가적인, 추가적인 |
| provide | v. 제공하다, 공급하다 |
| appreciate | v. 감사하다 |
| project | n. 계획사업, 프로젝트 |
| audiovisual | a. 시청각의 |
| equipment | n. 장치, 장비 |
| describe | v. 묘사하다 |
| location | n. 위치, 장소 |
| convenient | a. 편리한 |
| efficient | a. 효율적인 |
| client | n. 고객 |
| deadline | n. 마감일, 기한 |
| stationery | n. 문구류 |
| coordinator | n. 조정자, 진행자, 코디네이터 |
| cater | v. 음식을 제공하다 |

- approximately — ad. 대체로, 대략적으로
- hesitate — v. 망설이다
- assistance — n. 원조, 조력
- investment — n. 투자
- accommodation — n. 숙박시설, 적응
- explore — v. 탐구하다
- single — a. 하나의
- tentative — a. 임시적인, 잠정적인
- agenda — n. 의제
- attendee — n. 참석자
- brochure — n. 소책자, 브로셔
- estimate — v. 추정하다, 평가하다 n. 견적서, 견적
- praise — v. 칭찬하다
- immediately — ad. 즉시
- encourage — v. 장려하다
- acknowledge — v. 승인하다, 인식하다, 인정하다
- correspondence — n. 서한, 서신
- offer — v. 제공하다 n. 제공, 제안
- faculty — n. 교수진
- contact — v. 연락하다, 접촉하다 n. 연락, 접촉
- public relations — n. 홍보
- return — v. 돌려주다, 되돌리다
- entitle — v. ~라고 칭하다, 이름 붙이다, 자격을 주다
- banquet — n. 연회
- indicate — v. 가리키다, 지시하다
- liability — n. 부채, 책임, 의무
- insurance — n. 보험
- annual — a. 일년의
- working out — v. (계획등을) 만들어내다
- referent — a. 관계의, 엄습한(to)
- reserve — v. 예약하다, 유보하다
- executive — n. 임원 a. 임원의, 간부의
- vendor — n. 판매자, 상인

## 서비스 요청 편지

**Highspeed Auto Services**

56 Moorefield Hill CT.

Vienna, VA 32230

(703) 885-6334, FAX (703) 885-6330

May 12, 2007

Ms. Emma Watson
Cherish Conference Center
314 Golden Lane
Fairfax, VA 11270

Dear Ms. Watson:

In our telephone conversation on yesterday, we discussed plans for our meeting at your conference center. I would like to confirm these plans.

The meeting will be from July 18 to 19. We will need two rooms. Seventy people will attend the meeting.

I have additional requests:

- Could you provide six tables for each room?
- Is it possible to have a laptop and a beam projector in one room?
- Is it possible to have an OHP in another room?
- Would you be able to serve lunch on the 18th?

I would appreciate your answers by next Tuesday. If you need any more information, please call me.

I would like to thank you for your help in planning our meeting.

Sincerely yours,

Spencer Jones
Public Relations Manager

SJ/hs

다음 질문에 적절한 답을 고르시오.

1. 이 편지를 쓴 사람은?

ⓐ Spencer Jones ⓑ Emma Watson

2. 이 편지를 받는 사람은?

ⓐ Spencer Jones ⓑ Emma Watson

3. Mr. Jones가 일하는 곳의 위치는?

ⓐ Vienna, VA ⓑ Fairfax, VA

4. 어떤 시청각 자료를 요청하고 있는가?

ⓐ microphone ⓑ OHP

5. 부가적인 요청사항은 무엇인지 모두 쓰시오.

ⓐ ____________ ⓑ ____________

ⓒ ____________ ⓓ ____________

## 서비스 제공 확인 편지

**Cherish Conference Center**
314 Golden Lane
Fairfax, VA 11270
(703) 756-8822, Fax (703) 756-8823

May 15, 2007

Mr. Spencer Jones
Public Relations Manager
Highspeed Auto Services
56 Moorefield Hill CT.
Vienna, VA 32230

Dear Mr. Jones:

Thank you for your May 12 letter expressing interest in the Cherish Conference Center. This letter will confirm our plans for your meeting.

We understand that your company would like to reserve two rooms from July 18 to July 19. Approximately seventy people will attend your meeting.

As you requested, we will provide twelve-six tables in each room. We will also have a laptop and a beam projector available in one room. We will provide an OHP in another room. We will serve lunch on the 18th.

If you have any questions or need to make any changes, please contact me immediately.

We look forward to seeing you on July 18.
Sincerely yours,

Emma Watson
Meeting Planner

cc : K. Chen, Multimedia Department

EW/kk

## 적절한 답을 고르시오.

1. 누가 Mr. Jones이 요청한 회의를 준비하고 있는가?

ⓐ Mr. Bond ⓑ Ms. Watson

2. Ms. Watson이 편지를 작성한 날짜는?

ⓐ May 12 ⓑ May 15

3. 이 편지를 쓴 목적은 무엇인가?

ⓐ To reserve two rooms

ⓑ To confirm information

4. Mr. Jones가 이 편지의 내용과 다른 변경 사항이 생겼을 때 할 일은?

5. 회의가 개최될 장소는?

ⓐ Vienna ⓑ Fairfax

6. 이 편지의 참조인은?

ⓐ K. Chen ⓑ E. Watson

## 서비스 요청 편지의 작성 방법

**1. 편지를 쓰는 목적이나 경위를 설명한다.**

Ex I read your advertisement in the newspaper.

OR

This will confirm our telephone conversation.

**2. 요청사항을 밝힌다.**

Ex We will need the following:

OR

Can you provide the following?

**3. 기한을 명시한다.**

Ex I would appreciate your answer by next Tuesday.

OR

We would like to have your answer by June 5.

**4. 추가적인 정보를 부탁하고, 수신자에게 감사를 표현한다.**

Ex If you need more information, please call.

OR

I appreciate your help.

## 서비스 제공을 확인하는 편지의 작성 방법

서비스 제공을 확인하는 편지를 작성하는 목적은 다음과 같다.

① 서비스 요청이 잘 접수되었음을 알려준다.
② 요청에 대한 세부사항을 다시 확인해 준다.
③ 우호관계를 형성하고 반복적인 거래를 유도한다.

**1. 편지를 잘 받았음을 알린다.**

Ex Thank you for your letter of May 12.

OR

This will confirm our telephone conversation.

**2. 서비스 내용에 대해 재확인한다.**

Ex We understand that you would like the following.

OR

As you requested, we will provide the following:

**3. 추가적인 도움을 제공할 것을 약속한다.**

Ex If you have any questions, please call.

OR

We look forward to seeing you next month.

## 비즈니스 실례 : '체크리스트' 사용하기

비슷한 종류의 서비스를 반복해서 제공할 때에는 '체크리스트'를 만들어서 사용하면 더 편리하고 효율적으로 업무를 할 수 있다.

Cherish Conference Center는 회의실 예약을 접수할 때 아래와 같은 '체크리스트'를 사용한다. 6 페이지의 견본 편지를 참조하여, 다음의 '체크리스트'를 완성하시오.

**Cherish Conference Center**

314 Golden Lane

Fairfax, VA 11270

(703) 756-8822 · Fax (703) 756-8823

**CHECKLIST**

Company : ______________________________

Meeting Location : ______________________________

Date(s) : Arrival Date ______________ Time : ______________

Departure Date ______________ Time : ______________

Number of attendants :

□ 2-10 □ 51-100 □ Other ________

□ 11-50 □ 101-150

Room Requirements : ______________________________

Required Equipments :

□ Microphone □ Laptop □ OHP

□ Beam projector □ TV/VCR

Seating :

Tables ______________________________

Catering :

□ Breakfast □ Lunch □ Reception

□ Morning coffee □ Afternoon coffee □ Dinner

Contact :

Name : ______________________________

Department : ______________ Title : ______________

Telephone : ______________ Fax : ______________

Mobile Phone : ______________ E-Mail : ______________

## 문법 따라잡기(I) : 의문문의 유형

영어에는 조동사로 시작하는 Yes/No 의문문과 의문사로 시작하는 의문문의 두 가지 유형이 있다.

### 1. 조동사로 시작하는 Yes/No 의문문

| 조동사 | 주어 | 동사+......? | 대답 |
|---|---|---|---|
| Do | you | have the book? | Yes, I do. |
| Is | the seminar | confirmed for Tuesday, July 22? | No, it isn't. |
| Can | you | send me the data? | Yes, I can. |
| Would | you | call me tomorrow? | Yes, I would. |

### 적절한 답을 고르시오.

**1.** Did you finish your homework?

ⓐ Yes, I did. ⓑ Yes, I do.

**2.** Will he come until 10:00 P.M.?

ⓐ No, she isn't. ⓑ Yes, he will.

**3.** Has the table been ordered?

ⓐ Yes, it has. ⓑ Yes, it have.

**4.** Does Mr. Flant live in St. Louis?

ⓐ Yes, he does. ⓑ Yes, he did.

**5.** Could you plan the event?

ⓐ No, I couldn't. ⓑ No, I won't.

6. Can you meet the deadline?

ⓐ Yes, I can. ⓑ No, I didn't.

7. May we leave a vacation?

ⓐ Yes, you may. ⓑ No, you don't.

8. Did you attend the party?

ⓐ Yes, I will. ⓑ Yes, I did.

9. Has he left already?

ⓐ Yes, he did. ⓑ No, he hasn't.

10. Do you need her support?

ⓐ No, you won't. ⓑ No, I don't.

## 2. 의문사로 시작하는 의문문

| 의문사 | 조동사+주어? |
|---|---|
| What | is the subject? |
| When | is the meeting? |
| Who | is the new employee? |
| Where | will the conference be held? |

➡

| 대답 |
|---|
| It is Business Correspondence. |
| On July 25. |
| Keith Owen. |
| In the Grand Ball Room. |

보기 중에서 적절한 의문사를 골라 밑줄을 채우시오.

| How many | What | How long | Where | When | Who |
|---|---|---|---|---|---|

Example Who is Keith Owen?
He is a new employee.

1. ____________ does the class start?
It begins on Tuesday, April 2 at 7 p.m.

2. ____________ stationery is needed?

Laser pointer and post-it.

3. ____________ will the meeting be held?

At the Johnson Conference Center.

4. ____________ clients will attend?

Thirty clients will attend.

5. ____________ will the meeting last?

For three days, from March 10 to 12.

기한을 명시하고, 또 준수하는 것은 비즈니스의 중요한 부분이다. 상대방에게 기한을 정해 주면, 더 정확하고 질높은 서비스를 기대할 수 있다.

You must submit the report by tomorrow at 11 a.m.
Your deadline is next Monday morning.

## 문법 따라잡기(II) : 대명사

이미 언급되었던 사람이나 사물을 다시 받을 때에 대명사를 사용한다.

| 주격 대명사 | | 목적격 대명사 | |
|---|---|---|---|
| I | we | me | us |
| you | you | you | you |
| he | they | him | them |
| she | | her | |
| it | | it | |

Exercise 다음의 질문에 답하시오.

Ex

Mr. Chapmen is my boss. He has worked here for ten years.

대명사는? He

대명사가 지칭하는 것은? Mr. Chapmen

1. The President read the letter.

   He called his secretary.

   대명사는? ____________

   대명사가 지칭하는 것은? ____________

2. The manager turned on the computer.

   He wrote a report.

   대명사는? ____________

   대명사가 지칭하는 것은? ____________

3. The executives planned their Seminar.

   They will meet on October 12.

   대명사는? ____________

   대명사가 지칭하는 것은? ____________

4. The vendor sent the bill.

She mistyped the total amount.

대명사는? ___________

대명사가 지칭하는 것은? ___________

Exercise 다음의 밑줄 친 문장들을 올바른 목적격 대명사를 넣어서 완성하시오(대명사가 받아야 할 단어는 굵은 글자체로 되어 있음).

Ex

We need these **letters** typed today.

Can you type <u>them</u> before 5 p.m.?

1. The **meeting planners** didn't arrive until 10 a.m.

We wanted ___________ to come earlier.

2. **He** received the books.

The books were sent to ___________.

3. I received your **bill**.

I put ___________ in the file.

4. **Maggie** looked the telephone message.

Ask ___________ what the number was.

5. **She** cancelled the reservation.

The restaurant could not give ___________ enough seats.

| 소유격 (한정사) | | 소유 대명사 | |
|---|---|---|---|
| my | our | mine | ours |
| your | your | yours | yours |
| her | their | hers | theirs |
| his | | his | |
| its | | its | |

Exercise 적절한 답을 고르시오.

1. ( We , Our ) meal will be served shortly.

2. These notebooks are ( my , mine ).

3. ( Mine , My ) company's name is MK Corporation.

4. This document was completed by ( him , his ).

5. ( My , Mine) parents expected me to be a doctor.

6. ( Their , Theirs ) staff meeting will be at the meeting room.

7. ( Her , Hers ) bags are missing.

8. This file is ( your , yours ).

9. These duties are ( ours , our ).

10. I borrowed ( their , theirs ) tools.

## 문법 따라잡기(III) - 물음표와 마침표

| 물음표 | 마침표 |
|---|---|
| 의문문의 마지막에 물음표(?) 사용 | 평서문의 마지막에 마침표(.) 사용 |
| What color do you like?<br>Do you have any questions?<br>What equipment will you need? | She is from singapore.<br>If you have any questions please call.<br>We will need ten copies of this report. |

### 1. 물음표(?)

❶ 직접의문문 뒤에 물음표를 사용한다.

Why was the delay caused?

When will you be ready?

❷ 부가의문문 다음에 물음표를 사용한다.

She plans to transfer the position soon, doesn't she?

You read the notice, didn't you?

❸ 한 문장 내에서도 질문이 나열될 때에는 질문마다 물음표를 삽입한다.

Who got promoted? - Elisabeth? Linda? Tony?

Is the correct punctuation mark a period? a comma? a question mark?

### 2. 마침표(.)

마침표는 문장의 마지막에 '완전히 멈춤'이라는 표시이다.

❶ 평서문 또는 명령문 다음에 마침표를 찍는다.

My boss went to the business trip.

Please answer my question.

❷ 간접 화법으로 의문문을 나다낼 때에는 마침표를 사용헌다.

Mr. Sandler asked if he could help Nancy.

The manager inquired whether there would be a fee for the service.

③ 정중한 부탁을 의미할 때는 의문문의 형태이더라도 마침표를 사용한다. 이러한 종류의 문장은 주로 비즈니스 서신의 마지막 문장이나 문단에서 볼 수 있다(최근에는 물음표를 사용하는 경우도 있다.).

Could you please confirm the reservation.

May I have your name.

④ 약어나 이니셜에도 마침표를 사용한다.

T. S. Eliot / Rev. Cooper / 2:30 p.m.

## 예제 1

다음의 편지를 읽고, 적절한 곳에 물음표나 마침표를 삽입하시오.

LUTHER CONFERENCE CENTER
50 Rockefeller Plaza
New York, NY 12330
212-335-6633 · FAX 212-335-6655

October 25, 2007

Eunice Lee
Project Coordinator
ULI Co., Ltd.
56 Kindle Center
New Haven, Connecticut 07335

Dear Ms. Lee:

Thank you for your telephone call this morning

Luther Conference Center is pleased to plan your next meeting Could you please answer the following questions

How many rooms will you require
How many people will attend your meeting
What are the dates of the meeting
How long will the meeting lasts
What audio-visual equipment will you require
Which meals would you like be catered

I look forward to hearing from you

Sincerely yours,

Shannon Davidson
Meeting Planner

SD/rs

## 예제 2

다음 편지를 읽고 문법적인 오류나 잘못된 부분을 찾아서 고치시오.

**Sunnyvale Conference Center**

333 East Park Avenue · Sunnyvale, CA 91330 Tel/414-664-7702 Fax/414-663-7720

August 19, 2007

Chandler Brown Mr.
A&P Publishing Company
2300 James Stret
Atlanta, Georgia 30341

Mr. Brown Dear:

Thank your for your June 12 telephone call expressing interest in Conference Center. This letter will confirm our Sunnyvale plans for your meeting.

we understand that your company would like to reserve two rooms at our facilities from August 20 to August 21. Approximately 100 people will attend your meeting.

As you requested, we will provide ten tables-five in each room. All of the rooms have a microphone, a slide projector and a beam projector. Us will serve morning coffee and lunch on both days.

if you have any questions or need to make any changes, please contact me immediately?

We looks forward to seeing you on August 20.

Sincerely,

Mario Lopez
Project Manager
KP/jk

## 예제 3

다음 편지에서 문법적으로 오류가 있는 곳을 찾아서 바르게 고치시오.

**MEGA RENTAL SERVICES**

1234 Main Street, Suite 5

Businessville, OK 55342

553-9987

May 20, 2007

Mr. Andre Grant
Rockefeller Conference Center
223 Huntington
New York, new york 10019

Dear Lee Mr.:

in our telephone conversation of May 19, 2007, we discussed plans for our meeting at your conference center. I want to confirm these plans.

The meeting will be from June 15 to 17, 2004? We will need 4 rooms. Approximately 60 people will attend the meeting. We will need microphones in each room, we will only serve coffee at the breaks coffee.

We have additional requests:
It is possible to have a laptop and beam projector in each room?
Is it possible to have an OHP in one room?
Would you be able to serve lunch on the 17th?

Could you please respond to these requests by May 28, 2007.
If you need any more information, please call me.

I appreciate your help in planning our meeting.

Sincerely yours,

Roger Moore
Special Projects

AG/rm

## 예제 4

Rockefeller Conference Center에서는 하단의 편지를 참조하여 다음과 같은 '체크리스트'를 작성하였다. 아래의 보기 중에서 알맞은 단어를 골라 원본 편지의 밑줄을 채우시오.

**Checklist**

Company : Esther Arden Cosmetics
Meeting location : Rockefeller Conf. Center
Date : December 10-13
No. of people attending : About 150
No. of rooms : 10
Audio-visual equipment : Microphones / Simultaneous translation
Catering : Coffee breaks

November, attend, by, hesitate, plans, to, requests, conversation microphone, breaks, room, questions, confirm, in, meeting

**Esther Arden Cosmetics**

63 Foxhall Crescent
Missoula, Montana 30567
406-885-9909
Fax 406-886-9988

October 2, 2007

Andre Grant
Rockefeller Conference Center
50 Rockefeller Plaza
New York, New york 10019

Dear Mr. Grant:

In our telephone ______ of August 19, 2007, we discussed ______ for our ______ at your conference center. I would like to _____ these plans.

The meeting will be from _____ 10-13, 2007. We will need 10 _____.
Approximately 150 people will _____ the meeting.

We have additional _____:

Is it possible to have a _____ and simultaneous translation service in each room?
Would you be able _____ serve coffee at the coffee _____ ?

Could you please respond _____ early next week? Do not _____ to call me if you have any _____.

I appreciate your assistance _____ planning this meeting.

Sincerely yours,

Karl Trever
Customer Service Representative

## 예제 5

다음의 '체크리스트'를 참조하여, 다음 페이지의 공란에 Lehman Investment Company의 Robert Park이 Schumidt Conference Center의 Mandy McDonald 에게 보내는 편지를 작성하시오.

# Schmidt Conference Center

238 Bellevue Street
Vienna, VA 20443
(703) 945-3344 · Fax (703) 945-3355

## CHECKLIST

Company : Lehman Investment Company

Meeting Location : Schmidt Conference Center at Vienna

Date(s) : Arrival Date Dec. 15 Time : 09:00

Departure Date Dec. 18 Time : 17:00

Number attendants :

☐ 2-10 ☐ 51-100 ☑ Other 170

☐ 11-50 ☐ 101-150

Room Requirements : 2

Required Equipments :

☑ Microphone ☐ Tape recorder ☐ OHP

☑ Beam projector ☐ TV/VCR

☑ Simultaneous Translation Booth.

Seating :

Tables 10 - 5 in each room

Catering :

☐ Breakfast ☑ Lunch ☐ Reception

☐ Morning coffee ☑ Afternoon coffee ☐ Dinner

Contact :

Name : Robert Park

Department : Accounting Dept.

Telephone : (703) 266-3300 Fax : (703) 266-3301

Mobile Phone : (555) 737-3903 E-Mail : lchang@Lehman.com

316 Wilson Boulevard Arlington, Virginia 22200 (703) 266-3300

**Lehman Investment Company**

## 예제 6

귀하가 Ms. Parker의 비서라고 가정하자. 귀하의 상사는 아래와 같은 지시와 고객의 명함을 남겼다. 아래의 '체크리스트'를 참조하여, 다음 페이지에 적절한 편지를 작성하시오.

**귀하의 상사가 남긴 메모**

**From the desk of Sherman Parker**

Meeting Planner

Write a letter to Mr. Shaw and confirm our conversation of 4/19/07.
Here's his business card.

**고객의 명함**

**Mr. Albert Shaw**
Managing Director, Public Relations

MSK Construction, Inc.
4711 East Road
Atlanta, Georgia 33341
(404) 555-3100, Fax (404) 555-3000

**K2 Conference Center**

Route 28, Mountainside
New Jersey 07791
(311) 916-2277 · Fax (311) 916-2200

Checklist

Company : MSK Construction, Inc.
Meeting Location : K2 Conference Center at New Jersey
Date(s) : Arrival Date June 13 Time : 9:00 a.m.
Departure Date June 15 Time : 5:00 p.m.

Number of attendants
☐ 2-10 ☐ 51-100 ☑ Other 190
☐ 11-50 ☐ 101-150

Room Requirements : 4

Required Equipments :
☑ Microphone ☐ Tape recorder ☐ OHP
☑ Beam projector ☐ TV/VCR

Seating :
Tables 8 (2 in each room)

Catering :
☑ Breakfast (6/13+15) ☑ Lunch ☐ Reception
☐ Morning coffee ☑ Afternoon coffee ☐ Dinner

Contact :
Name : Mr. Albert Shaw
Department : Public Relations Title : Managing Director
Telephone : (404) 555-3100 Fax : (404) 555-3000
Mobile Phone : (303) 222-3100 E-Mail : ashaw@msk.com

**K2 Conference Center**

Route 28, Mountainside
New Jersey 07791
(311) 916-2277 · Fax (311) 916-2200

## 예제 7

다음의 편지를 해석하시오.

Dear Mr. Simpson :

Thank you for signing and returning Contract #305-1, which entitles you to use the banquet facilities at Grand Hall on December 10. As the agreement indicates, you will be responsible for liability insurance during the time of the banquet.

I look forward to planning the banquet menu and to working out other details that will make your company's annual dinner a real success for all 500 guests.

Yours sincerely,

해석

## 예제 8

다음 편지를 해석하시오.

FUTURE CONSTRUCTION COMPANY

88 Oakwood Terrace · Elgin, Illinois 60303 · 315-333-6886

November 18, 2007

Ms. Cindy Graco
Convention Manager
Little Cabin Inn
200 Irving Lane
Little Creek, CA 92358

Dear Ms. Graco:

SUBJECT : ACCOMMODATIONS FOR ANNUAL CONFERENCE

We would like to explore the possibility of holding next year's Regional Construction Conference at the Little Cabin Inn. Our meeting is scheduled from Sunday, February 16, to Saturday, February 22. We will require single rooms for a minimum of 190 employees and guests for the entire week.

Our needs for meeting rooms are described in the enclosed tentative agenda for our week-long conference. The times of the meetings, breaks, and meals are specified in this agenda, as well as the approximate number of attendees for each session.

Will you please provide us with brochures and pamphlets describing your room accommodations, dining facilities, and sports and recreational facilities? Also, please suggest menus for the scheduled lunches and dinners that are listed on the enclosed agendas and estimate the approximate cost per person for both the rooms and the meals.

After we review your brochures and estimates, I would like to visit the Little Cabin Inn so that I may have the pleasure of seeing your highly praised resort.

Sincerely yours,

Gary Monroe
Regional Representative

Enclosure

해석

UNIT 02

# Ordering & Acknowledging an Order

(상품 주문 및 접수 편지)

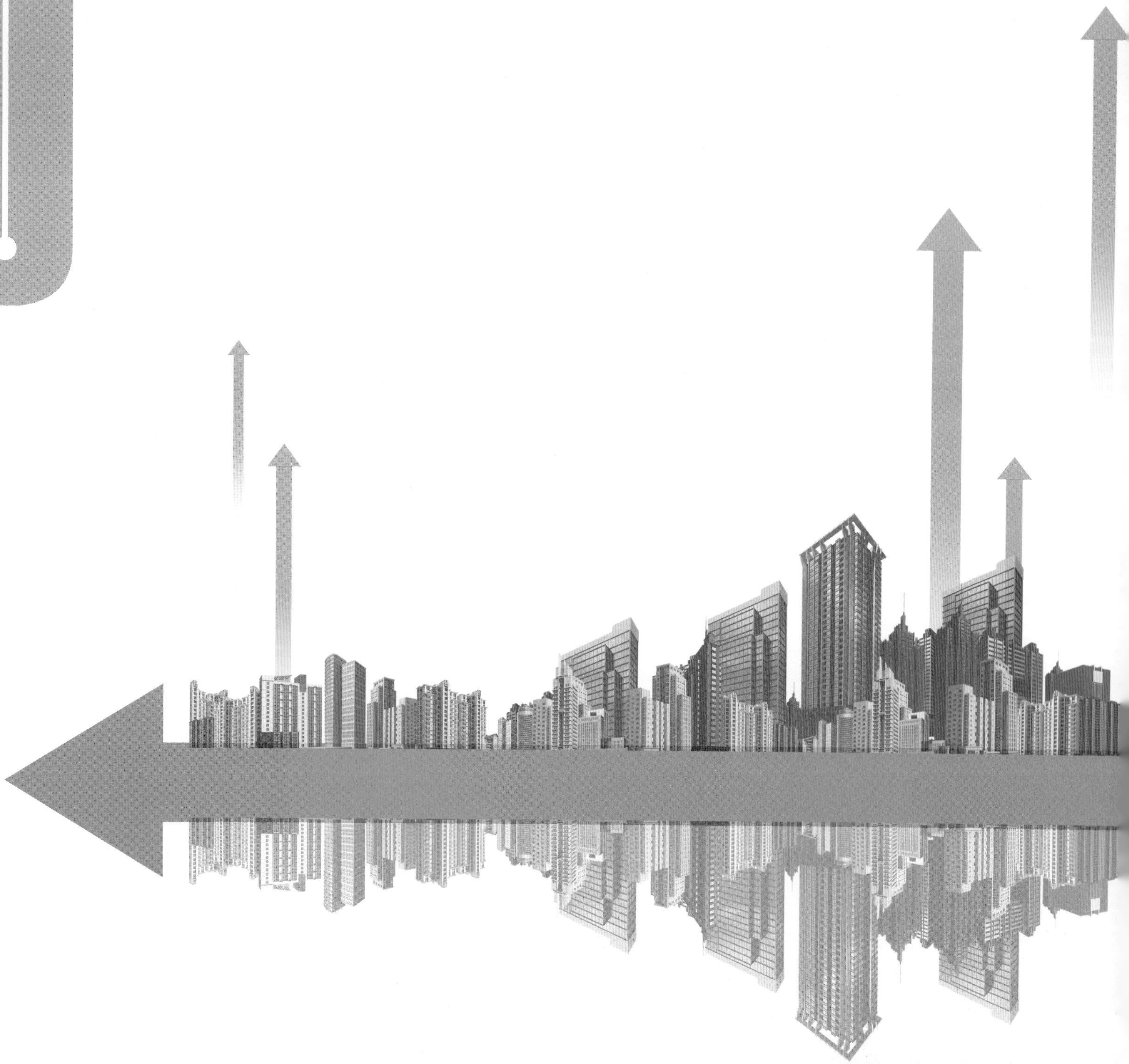

UNIT 02

# Ordering & Acknowledging an Order
(상품 주문 및 접수 편지)

## 어휘 학습

- supply — v. 공급하다 n. (주로 복수형으로 쓰여서) 물품, 비품
- promotional — a. 홍보의, 판촉의
- packet — n. 소포, 한 묶음
- initial — a. 최초의, 시작의
- according to — (숙어) ~에 따르면
- unit price — n. 단가 (한 개의 가격), 단위당 가격
- quantity — n. 양, 수량 (반. quality)
- handling — (동명사/현재분사) 취급, 관리 (v. handle)
- down payment — n. 계약금, 선급금, 착수금
- remainder — n. 나머지, 잔여
- forward — v. 전달하다 ad. 앞으로
- courtesy — n. 공손, 예의바름
- processing — (동명사/현재분사) 처리
- anticipate — v. ①기대하다, 고대하다 ②예상하다
- receipt — n. 영수증

| | |
|---|---|
| • recipient | n. 수신자, 받는 사람 |
| • easy-to-read | a. 읽기 쉬운 |
| • purchase order | n. 구매요청서, 구매지시서 |
| • format | n. 형태, 모양 |
| • accompany | v. 함께하다, 수행하다, 동반하다 |
| • accounting | n. 회계 |
| • delivery | v. 배달, 배송 |
| • prompt | a. 즉각적인 |
| • availability | n. 가능성, 가능함 |
| • replacement | n. 대체, 대안 |
| • encourage | v. 장려하다, 독려하다 |
| • enumeration | n. 목록, 일람표 |
| • emphasis | n. 강조 (v. emphasize) |
| • supervisor | n. 감독관, 상사 |
| • confirmation | n. 확인 (v. confirm 확인하다, 입증하다) |
| • alternate | v. 교체하다, 대체하다 a.교체의, 대안의<br>(n. alternative 대안) |
| • convenience | n. 편리 (a. convenient) |
| • enthusiastically | ad. 열정적으로 |
| • be made of | (숙어) ~으로 만들어지다 |
| • relationship | n. 관계 |
| • substitution | n. 대리, 대체 |
| • dealer | n. 상인, 업자 |
| • affecting | a. 감동적인, 영향을 미치는 |
| • budget | n. 예산 |
| • invoice | n. (화물을 보낼 때 쓰는) 인보이스, 송장(送狀), 청구서 |
| • in stock | 재고가 있는 (반. out of stock = sold out) |
| • back order | ①이월 주문 / ②이월 주문하다 |

## 상품을 주문하는 편지

534 East Ventura Blvd., Encino, CA 99710, 818/553-9900 Fax : 818/553-9911

**FYC SUPPLIES**

February 25, 2007

Ward Merchandise
656 S. 3600 West
Salt Lake City, UT 84120

Ladies and Gentlemen :

We received your promotional packet and would like to place an initial order for the following merchandise. Item numbers and prices are according to your price list of December, 2006.

| Item No. | Item name | Unit Price | Q'ty | Total |
|---|---|---|---|---|
| 33514 | Correction pen | 2.89 | 250 | $722.50 |
| 33496 | Paper clip | 7.99/Box | 72Boxes | 575.28 |
| 32584 | Post-it | 1.39 | 1000 | 1,390.00 |
| | | | | $2,687.78 |
| Tax | | | | 174.71 |
| Shipping & Handling | | | | 54.50 |
| TOTAL | | | | $2,916.99 |

The required 10% down payment of $291.70 is enclosed. The remainder will be forwarded upon receipt of goods.

Any courtesy you can offer us in processing this order will be appreciated. We anticipate doing much more business with you in the future.

Very truly yours,

Terry Woods
Purchasing Manager

TW/jm

## 적절한 답을 고르시오.

**1.** 이 편지를 쓴 목적은 무엇인가?

ⓐ 상품을 보내기 위해

ⓑ 요금을 지불하기 위해

ⓒ 상품을 주문하려고

ⓓ 안부를 전하기 위해

**2.** 편지 내용에 따르면, Ms. Woods는 다음에 다시 또 Ward Merchandise와 거래하고 싶어하는가?

ⓐ Yes ⓑ No ⓒ Not certain

**3.** Ms. Woods가 상품을 받고 나면 얼마를 송금해야 하는가?

ⓐ $291.70 ⓑ $2,687.78

ⓒ $2,916.99 ⓓ $2,625.29

**4.** 이 편지의 수신자가 편지를 받은 후에 할 조치는 다음 중 무엇인가?

ⓐ 편지를 잘 받았음을 알린다.

ⓑ 상품을 발송한다.

ⓒ 상품을 이월주문한다.

ⓓ 청구서를 보낸다.

## 주문을 접수하는 편지

**Ward Merchandise**

656 S. 3600 West

Salt Lake City, UT 84120

February 28, 2007

Terry Woods

Purchasing Manager

FYC Supplies

534 East Ventura Blvd.

Encino, CA 99710

Dear Ms. Woods:

Thank you very much for your order of February 25, 2007. All the items you ordered are in stock. Therefore, they are being processed and will be shipped by Tuesday, March 4, 2007. Also, we appreciate very much for the down payment of $291.70.

We appreciate your business and look forward to serving you in the future.

Sincerely yours,

Maria Owen

Shipping Clerk

## 적절한 답을 고르시오.

1. 물품을 주문한 사람은 누구인가?

ⓐ Terry Woods

ⓑ Maria Owen

2. Maria Owen이 소속되어 있는 회사는?

ⓐ FYC Supplies

ⓑ Ward Merchandise

3. 물품이 배송될 날짜는?

______________________

4. 이 편지를 쓴 사람의 어투는?

ⓐ 중립적

ⓑ 우호적

## 편지의 구조 – 상품 주문

'주문 편지'란 상품을 구매하기 위해 작성하는 편지를 일컫고, 회사의 제품을 안내하는 책자는 '카달로그'나 '브로셔'라고 하며, 상품을 구매하기 위해 필요한 정보를 기입할 수 있도록 만들어 놓은 양식을 구매요청서(Purchase Order 또는 P.O.)라 부른다.
준비해 놓은 구매요청서가 없는 경우에는 주문편지에 관련 정보를 모두 포함해야 한다.

**1. 주문을 하고 싶다는 문장으로 본문을 시작한다.**

Ex We would like to place an initial order for the following merchandise.

**2. 주문하려는 상품에 대해 알린다.**

Ex Item numbers and quantity are listed as below.

**3. 상품에 대한 상세정보를 알아보기 쉬운 형태로 제시**

Ex

| Item# | Name | Unit Price | Q'ty | Total |
|---|---|---|---|---|
| . | . | . | . | . |
| . | . | . | . | . |

**4. 배송을 원하는 시기, 장소, 방법 등에 대해 명시한다.**

Ex We would like to receive the merchandise as soon as possible.

## 1. 주문 절차

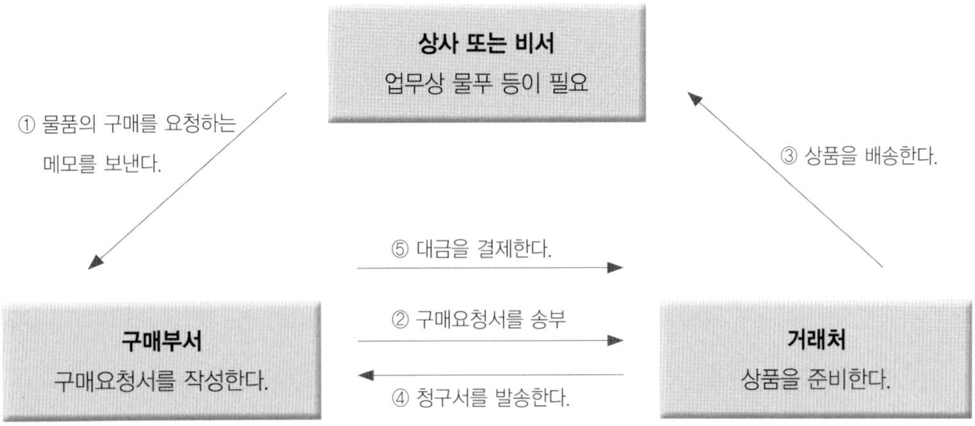
상사 또는 비서
업무상 물푸 등이 필요
① 물품의 구매를 요청하는 메모를 보낸다.
구매부서
구매요청서를 작성한다.
⑤ 대금을 결제한다.
② 구매요청서를 송부
④ 청구서를 발송한다.
거래처
상품을 준비한다.
③ 상품을 배송한다.

POST

다음의 대화에서 Joan은 신입사원이며, 회사 업무상으로 소모품을 구입하려고 한다. 선배 사원인 George에게 구매절차에 대해 문의하고 있다.

Joan : George, I need some stationery - like pens and notebooks.

Geroge : Write a memo to the Purchasing Department to order them, Joan.

Joan : Can't we just buy some supplies?

Geroge : No. We first have to write a memo to the Purchasing Department. They prepare a purchase order and send the purchase order to a vendor who sells office supplies.

Joan : Then what?

Geroge : The vendor ships the supplies to you, and sends bills to the Purchasing Department.

상자 안의 보기 중에서 적절한 단어를 골라 구매절차와 관련된 아래 문장들의 밑줄을 채우시오.

vendor, pay, supplies, bills, fax, purchase order, ships, accompanied, order

Ex Joan wants to ___________ pens and paper clips.

1. Joan and George need to order some ___________.

2. The Purchasing Department prepares a ___________.

3. The Purchase order will be ___________ by a cover letter.

4. The ___________ sells supplies.

5. The vendor ___________ the supplies.

6. The purchase order will be sent by ___________.

7. The vendor ___________ the company for the supplies.

8. The Purchasing Dept. will ___________ for the supplies.

## 편지의 구조 – 주문 접수

상품 주문 편지에 대한 답신을 '주문접수 편지'라고 한다. 이 편지의 목적은 다음의 내용들을 알리기 위해서이다.

1. 편지 수신
2. 주문 처리 과정
3. 상품 도착 일자

주문을 처리하고 상품을 배송하기 전에 이와 같은 편지를 보내는 이유는 (a) 우호관계를 형성하고, (b) 향후 주문을 지속적으로 받게 장려하기 위함이다.

주문품을 문제없이 발송할 수 있을 때에는 다음의 순서를 따른다.

**1. 고객에게 감사 표현을 한다.**

Ex Thank you very much for your order of August 25.

↓

**2. 상품 발송 시기와 절차를 알린다.**

Ex They are being processed and will be shipped by Tuesday September 4.

↓

**3. 필요한 경우, 상세 주문 정보나 기타의 유의사항을 언급한다.**

Ex Also, we appreciate very much for the down payment of $165.30.

↓

**4. 우호관계를 형성한다.**

Ex We appreciate you for the order.

## 주문을 완벽하게 처리할 수 없을 때

주문을 처리하고 싶지만 때로는 다음과 같은 이유들 때문에 "죄송하지만, 귀하의 주문을 처리할 수 없습니다"라고 답해야 할 때가 있다.

❶ 고객의 주문이 불완전/부정확할 때
❷ 제품이 품절되었을 때
❸ 배송이 지연될 때

이러한 경우의 회신 편지를 쓸 때에는 다음과 같은 간접적인 표현을 사용한다.

❶ 먼저 고객의 주문에 대해 감사한다.
❷ 주문을 처리할 수 없는 이유에 대해 설명한다.
- 고객의 주문이 불완전하다면, 필요한 정보를 재요청한다.
- 제품이 품절되었다면, 대체품을 추천하거나 대안을 제시한다.
- 배송이 지연되면, 이유를 알리고 언제 어떻게 배송될 지에 대해 설명한다.

❸ 우호적인 마무리
- 제품을 다시 주문할 수 있도록 유도하는 문장을 사용한다.
- 고객만족이 당신(회사)의 최고 관심사라는 것을 알리면서 마무리하도록 한다.

## 주문을 거절할 때

어떤 주문은 불가피하게 거절해야 하는 경우도 있다. 귀사가 소매(고객과 직접 거래)영업은 하지 않는 도매점일 수도 있다. 이런 경우에는 고객이 대신 어디에서 주문할 수 있는지 알려 주고, 대리점에서 구입하는 것의 장점도 알려 준다.

## 구매 요청하는 메모

Joan은 구매부서의 Young-Ki Kim에게 다음의 메모를 송부하였다.

**MEMORANDUM**

**To : Young-Ki Kim, Purchasing Dept.**
**From : Joan Young, Personnel Manager**
**Date : January 5, 2008**
**Subject : Supplies**
**Reference : Mitsuba Catalog Fall 2007**

**Please prepare a purchase order A.S.A.P for the following :**

| Item | Stock Number | Quantity | Unit Cost | Total Cost |
|---|---|---|---|---|
| Notebook | N370 | 4 | $2.5 | $10.00 |
| Diskette(3.5”) | P243 | 10box | $11.45/box | $114.50 |
| Laser Pointer | P240 | 10doz. | $11.45/doz. | $114.50 |

| | |
|---|---|
| **Subtotal** | **$ 239.00** |
| **Shipping & Handing** | **23.90** |
| **Total** | **$ 262.90** |

**Charge the total to the Personnel Dept.**

## 구매요청서

다음은 Joan의 메모를 받고 나서, Young-Ki Kim이 작성한 구매요청서이다.

East Rock Institute
6789 Main Street, Suite 10
Charity, MS. 23456
801) 555-4321

**PURCHASE ORDER**

**Vendor** : Mitsuba Corporation
234 South Eighth Street
New York, NY 10010

**Ship To** : Joan Young, Personnel Manager
(use above address unless otherwise indicated)

**Reference** : P.O. # 1127

**Bill To** : Young-Ki Kim, Purchasing Department
(use above address unless otherwise indicated)

**Delivery Date** : ASAP

| **Item** | **Stock Number** | **Quantity** | **Unit Cost** | **Total Cast** |
|---|---|---|---|---|
| Notebook | N370 | 4 | $2.5 | $10.00 |
| Diskette(3.5") | P243 | 10box | $11.45/box | $114.50 |
| Laser Pointer | P240 | 10doz. | $11.45/doz. | $114.50 |
| **Subtotal** | | | | **$239.00** |
| **Shipping/Handling (10%)** | | | | **$23.90** |
| **TOTAL** | | | | **$262.90** |

Prepared by : ____________ Approved by : ____________

Date prepared : ____________ Date approved : ____________

CC : Joan Young, Personnel / Accounting / Purchasing

위의 구매요청서를 참조하여, 다음 질문에 답하시오.

1. 물품은 누구에게 배송되는가?

2. 청구서를 받게 되는 부서와 담당자는?

3. 총 지불해야 하는 금액은 얼마인가?

4. 'Vendor'란 어떤 회사를 일컫는가?

5. Diskette(3.5")의 단가는 얼마인가?

6. 운송비는 얼마인가?

## 커버레터

좀 더 정중하고 구체적인 정보 전달을 위하여, 때때로 구매요청서와 함께 커버레터를 보내기도 한다. 커버레터란 함께 동봉된 것을 소개하는 편지라고 할 수 있다.
다음은 46 페이지의 구매 요청서와 함께 보내는 커버레터의 예이다.

East Rock Institute
6789 Main Street, Suite 10
Charity, MS. 23456
801) 555-4321

January 27, 2008

Mitsuba Corporation
234 South Eighth Street
New York, NY 10010

Ref : P.O. #1127

Dear Sir :

The purchase order referenced above is enclosed.

Please acknowledge the availability of the merchandise and expected delivery date. Also, please process the order as soon as possible. If you have any questions, please contact me.

Thank you for your prompt attention.

Sincerely yours,

Young-Ki Kim
Purchasing Clerk

Enclosure

## 주문을 완벽하게 처리할 수 없는 상황의 답변

**Ward Merchandise**

656 S. 3600 West
Salt Lake City, UT 84120

February 28. 2007

Mr.Terry Woods
Purchasing Manager
FYC Supplies
534 East Ventura Blvd.
Eucino, CA 99710

Dear Ms. Woods:

Thank you very much for your order of Feb. 25, 2007 and down payment of $ 291.70. Unfortunately, the item below is not in stock:

Item #33514 Correction Pen

We will back order this item and ship it within two(2) weeks.

The rest of your order is being processed and will be shipped by March 4, 2007.

Sincerely yours,

John Henry
Shipping Clerk

## 문법 따라잡기 : 대문자 표기(Capitalization)

단어의 첫 글자를 대문자로 하게 되면, 읽는 사람에게 새로운 내용이 시작된다거나 특정 인물, 장소나 사물을 지칭한다는 것을 환기시킬 수 있다.

(첫 글자) 대문자 사용의 일반적인 원칙은 다음과 같다.

❶ 특정 인물, 장소, 사물의 이름
❷ 문장의 첫 번째 단어
❸ 표제나 제목의 중요한 단어들

### 1. 사람의 이름

사람의 이름은 그 사람이 원하는 대로 쓰는 것이 가장 중요하다.

- Allison, Mrs. Sullivan

### 2. 장소명

주, 도시, 길, 공원, 강, 건물 이름 등의 고유명사의 단어 첫 글자를 대문자로 쓴다.

- Maine, Chicago, Main Street, Central Park, Mississippi River, Twin Building

Exercise 다음 문장에서 대문자 사용을 해야 하는 단어들에 밑줄을 치고, 그 이유를 설명하라.

1. Gina davis is an interesting young lady.

2. The entire family will move to the south because of Mr. mallon's new job.

**3**. The Nautilus traveled under the north pole.

**4**. When you travel to africa, you will surely want to visit moroco.

**5**. In France, you will enjoy visiting paris.

## 3. 조직, 회사, 기관 등의 이름과 브랜드/상품명

특정 회사, 협회, 위원회, 이사회 및 부서, 정당, 동창회, 동아리, 종교 집단 등의 단체명에 대문자를 사용한다.

- Our family belongs to the First Methodist Church.
- Our family attends the first church that was erected in this city.

어떤 단체명은 the로 시작되는데, the가 공식명의 일부분일 때는 대문자로 사용한다.

- Do you have an account with The Union Bank of California?
- That family has been reported to the Child Welfare Committee.

회사 이름 뿐만 아니라, 브랜드나 상품명 또한 대문자 사용이 적용된다.

- A new product, Liquiment, is made by the Russel Company.
- The new product, Liquiment, is a liquid cement.

## 4. 정부기관, 역사적 사건/문서

공공기관, 정부산하기관명 등에 대문자를 사용한다.

- Dr. Nick Patterson is employed by the Federal Bureau of Investigation.
- Dr. Nick Patterson turned the investigation over to the bureau that specializes in such problems.

역사적인 사건이나 중요한 문서들에 대문자를 사용한다.

Ex 시대, 전쟁, 법전 등; the Stone Age, World War II, the Bill of Rights, the Constitution, the Social Security Act.

## 5. 공휴일, 기념일, 명절 등

공휴일이나 특정 기념일 등에 대문자를 적용한다.

- New Year's Day, Christmas, National Education Week, Easter

*day*나 *week*도 기념일 이름의 일부분이면 함께 대문자화한다.

Exercise 다음 문장에서 대문자 사용을 해야 하는 단어들에 밑줄을 치고, 그 이유를 설명하라.

1. The department of labor will send you the data required.

2. What special activity is planned for secretary's week.

3. Did you see the declaration of independence in independence hall?

4. The baptist church is the only church in the community.

5. You are invited to spend thanksgiving day with our family.

## 6. 편지의 구두법

서두인사말(salutations)에서는, 문장의 첫 글자, 제목과 이름을 대문자로 쓴다.

Ex Dear Mr. Palmer:

결구(complimentary closings)에서는, 첫 글자만 대문자로 쓴다.

Ex Very truly yours,

### 7. 인쇄물의 표제나 제목의 각 단어들

인쇄물이나 서적 등의 제목의 각 단어 첫 글자는 대문자로 쓰지만, 다음의 단어들은 대문자로 쓰지 않는다.

- 관사: the, a, an
- 짧은 접속사(세 글자 이하) : and, as, but, if, or, nor
- 짧은 전치사(세 글자 이하) : at, by, for, in, of, off, on, out, to, up

- How to Become a Good Office Professional.
- Teaching Principles and Procedures for Gregg Shorthand.

### 8. 고유형용사

고유명사에서 파생된 형용사(고유형용사)는 대문자로 쓴다.

- Generally, American people are considered to be polite.
- Have you heard any of Wagnerian operas?

Exercise 다음 문장에서 대문자 사용을 해야 하는 단어들에 밑줄을 치고, 그 이유를 설명하라.

1. I have studied your pamphlet, how to invest and increase your holdings.

2. Do you expect to cross the mexican border on your trip?

3. Mr. Beck always uses the same complimentary closing-sincerely yours.

4. My new book, the business communication, will be published in next spring.

5. Purchase two copies of his latest book, information society by networking.

## 9. 인명과 함께 쓰이는 직책명

인명 앞에 쓰이는 직책명에 대문자를 사용한다.

- Special messages were sent from President Joseph O'mally, Professor Cathy Baker, and Kimberly Rogers.

사람 이름 뒤에 쓰이거나 이를 대신하는 고위 직책명을 대문자화한다.

- Bill Clinton, former President of the United States, also had served as the State Governor of Arkansas.

때로는 사람 이름 없이 사용된 직책명을 대문자로 쓴다.

- This report should be sent to the Dean immediately.

**Exercise** 다음 문장에서 대문자 사용을 해야 하는 단어들에 밑줄을 치고, 그 이유를 설명하라. 고칠 부분이 없으면 "C"라고 표시하시오.

1. When you visit seoul be sure to see the national assembly building.

2. Our case includes a judge, a jury, and a lawyer.

3. Principal wants to build a new dormitory.

4. The governor of our state attended a meeting with several other state governors.

5. Our association has given a $500 scholarship to a academically acheived student.

## 문법 따라잡기 : 숫자 표현 확인(Clarification)

비즈니스 서신에서 숫자를 표현할 때는, 풀어서 다시 쓰는 것이 좋다. 이렇게 반복하면 숫자 정보의 전달이 더 정확하게 된다.

| 수량의 숫자표현 | 문자표현 |
|---|---|
| 8 boxes<br>3 pieces | eight (8) boxes<br>three (3) pieces |

| 금액의 숫자표현 | 문자표현 |
|---|---|
| $ 9.45<br>$ 3,700 | nine dollars and forty-five cents ($9.45)<br>three thousand, seven hundred dollars ($3,700) |

예시

불명확 : Please give me seven (11) cartons of paper.
문자 (숫자)

명 확 : Do you want eleven (11) cartons of paper or seven (7) cartons of paper?
문자 (숫자) 문자 (숫자)

Exercise

1. 불명확 : We will need four (40) boxes of paper clips.
   명 확 : Do you want four (___) boxes of paper clips or forty (___) boxes of paper clips?
2. 불명확 : The shipping cost is five percent (6%) of the total.
   명 확 : Is the shipping cost ____ percent (___%) of the total or _____ percent (___%)?
3. 불명확: The total is seventy-two dollars ($ 7.20)
   명 확: Is the total seventy two dollars ($ ) or ___ dollars and _____ cents ($7.20)?

**기억하세요**

불명확한 숫자가 포함된 편지를 받으면, 다시 물어봐서 확인한다.
정확한 이해를 돕기 위하여 먼저 숫자를 문자로 풀어서 쓰고, 괄호 안에 숫자를 쓴다.

## 예제 1

아래의 보기에서 적절한 단어를 골라 다음 편지의 밑줄을 채우시오.

mutually, invoiced, date current interest, as, relationship, out, kind, line, enclosed, excited, on, at, doubled, to, via, for, confirmation, cover

Wakoviana

RAILROAD MODELS & ACCESSORIES
132 Cannonball Express
Flint, MI 53322
(505) 438-3092

June 27, 2007

Thomas Model Trains
4403 W.Magnolia Blvd.
Piedmont, VA 22301

Attn. : Peter Norton, Purchasing

Dear Mr. Norton:

Enclosed are the M-size tracks you orderd _____ phone _____ June 22, item number 84201. You will be invoiced under separate _____.

We are also including our _____ brochure, as the one from which you ordered is _____ of _____. Please note that our ______ of models and accessories has nearly ______ in the last two years. I think you will be very _____ about many of our new items.

Thank you ____ your order and your _____. We look forward to a long and _____ profitable _____.

Very truly yours,

Ellen Michelle
Vice President, Customer Service

EM:ot

## 예제 2

아래의 보기에서 적절한 단어를 골라 다음 편지의 밑줄을 채우시오.

substitution, toll-free, by, order, of, apologize, not, delay, free, prefer, placed, inconvenience, back, out of, in, note, ship

**FARMLAND INC**

Wholesale Agricultural Products
12443 Industrial Road
Topeka, KS 76509
(423) 687-4399

July 1, 2007

Mr. Chris Joseph Judd
2828 South Hills Place
Knoxville, TN 37917

Dear Mr. Judd:

Thank you for your _____ dated June 28.

Please _______ that items 10 and 11 (shovels and knives) are currently _______ stock and are, therefore, being _____ on _____ order. We expect to be able to _____ these items _____ July 15.

We _____ for the _____ and hope that it will not unduly _____ you. If you have any questions, or if you would _____ to make a _____ on these items, please feel _____ to call me at our _____ number: (800) 370-3389

Sincerely yours,

Michael M.Lorence

MML;sok

## 예제 3

38 페이지의 견본 주문 편지를 참조하여 그에 대한 회신을 작성하라.

귀하의 회사는 고객에게 직접 판매하지 않고, 전국적인 대리점을 통해 제품을 판매하기 때문에 고객의 주문을 직접 처리할 수 없다는 것과 아래의 대리점 주소와 연락처를 알려준다.
Slove Office Products, 4440 East Tropicana Avenue, Las Vegas, Nevada 89121.
Telephone number : (702) 555-2151.

**Ward Merchandise**

656 S. 3600 West
Salt Lake City, UT 84120
(280) 283-4088

## 예제 4

다음의 편지는 DLC Business Center가 Clean Source Company의 물품을 구매하기 위해서 보내는 편지이다. 이 편지를 읽고, 다음 페이지의 커버레터와 (그 다음) 페이지의 구매요청서로 나누어서 작성하시오.

**DLC Business Center**

23-75 Mountain Terrace, Twin Falls, ID 83301
Tel. (605) 808-2837, E-Mail. dlc_rep@dlc.org

December 12, 2007

Clean Source Company
190 Davis Street
San Francisco, CA 20210

Ladies and Gentlemen:

Please send me the following items from page 23 of your winter catalog:

| | | |
|---|---|---|
| 1 | Vacuum Cleaner 3000<br>Catalog No. CSC-600 | $210.00 |
| 1 | Replacement Filter<br>Catalog No. CSC-283 | 12.00 |
| | Shipping and Handling | 22.20 |
| | TOTAL | $244.20 |

Charge the order to my Master Card, M2735-2867-5889-23, which expires April 2010. Send the order to me at the address in the heading.

Sincerely yours,

Terry Woods

다음 공란에 ________ 페이지의 내용을 참조하여 커버레터를 작성하시오.

**DLC Business Center**

23-75 Mountain Terrace, Twin Falls, ID 83301
Tel. (605) 808-2837, E-Mail. dlc_rep@dlc.org

다음 공란에 ________ 페이지의 내용을 참조하여 구매요청서를 작성하시오.

**DLC Business Center**

23-75 Mountain Terrace, Twin Falls, ID 83301
Tel. (605) 808-2837, E-Mail. dlc_rep@dlc.org

## Purchase Order

**Vendor** :

**Ship To** :

**Reference** :

**Bill To** :

**Delivery Date** :

| Item | Stock Number | Quantity | Unit Cost | Total Cost |
|---|---|---|---|---|
| | | | | |

**Subtotal** ____________

**Shipping/Handling (10%)** ____________

**TOTAL** ____________

Prepared by : ________

Date prepared : ________

Approved by : ________

Date approved : ________

CC :

## 예제 5

58 페이지의 주문 편지를 참조하여 주문을 접수하는 답장을 작성하시오.

귀하는 주문품을 2007년 12월 18일까지 DHL을 통해 발송할 것이다.

CSC Clean Source Company

650 Davis street
San Francisco, CA 94111
(208) 770-8580

## 예제 6

아래와 같은 내용으로 주문 편지를 작성하시오.

주문하고자 하는 물품 : 10개의 CD Rewritable (단가 $3.90)

제품번호 : Catalog No. 570-A

수신처 : 123-A East Santa Monica Blvd. Los Angeles, CA 90012.

대금 지불 방법 : 제품을 받고 나서 바로 결제 (후불)

제품에 대해 알게 된 경로 : Photograph 잡지 9월호 38쪽의 광고를 통해서

**Nacon** Photographic Equipment

123-A East Santa Monica Blvd.

Los Angeles, CA 90012

TEL (330) 335-6677, FAX (330) 335-6688

## 예제 7

다음의 편지를 번역하시오.

**KFA Franchising Office**

12-22 Meredith Highway Columbia, MO 34321-6792

(309) 435-2668

August 26, 2007

Jonathan Jacobs
Cabot Lodge
Rt. 3, Box 12003
Portland, ME 02141

Dear Mr. Jacobs:

Your order #A-0811, dated August 19, was shipped via Overland Trucking Company on August 25 and should arrive within 6-10 working days.

As we mentioned in our conversation with you on Tuesday, one substitution was necessary to complete your order. The C-100 copier cartridge is no longer manufactured, and has been replaced with the upgraded C-100-X. This cartridge has nearly twice the capacity of the old C-100 at only $7 more per cartridge.

As we also discussed, we have reduced the cartridge order from 15 each to 10 each. All other items in the shipment are precisely as ordered.

We appreciate very much your continued patronage.

Yours truly,

Janice Theodore

JT:ds

번역

UNIT 03

# Claim Letter & Adjustment Letter

(배상요청 및 중재편지)

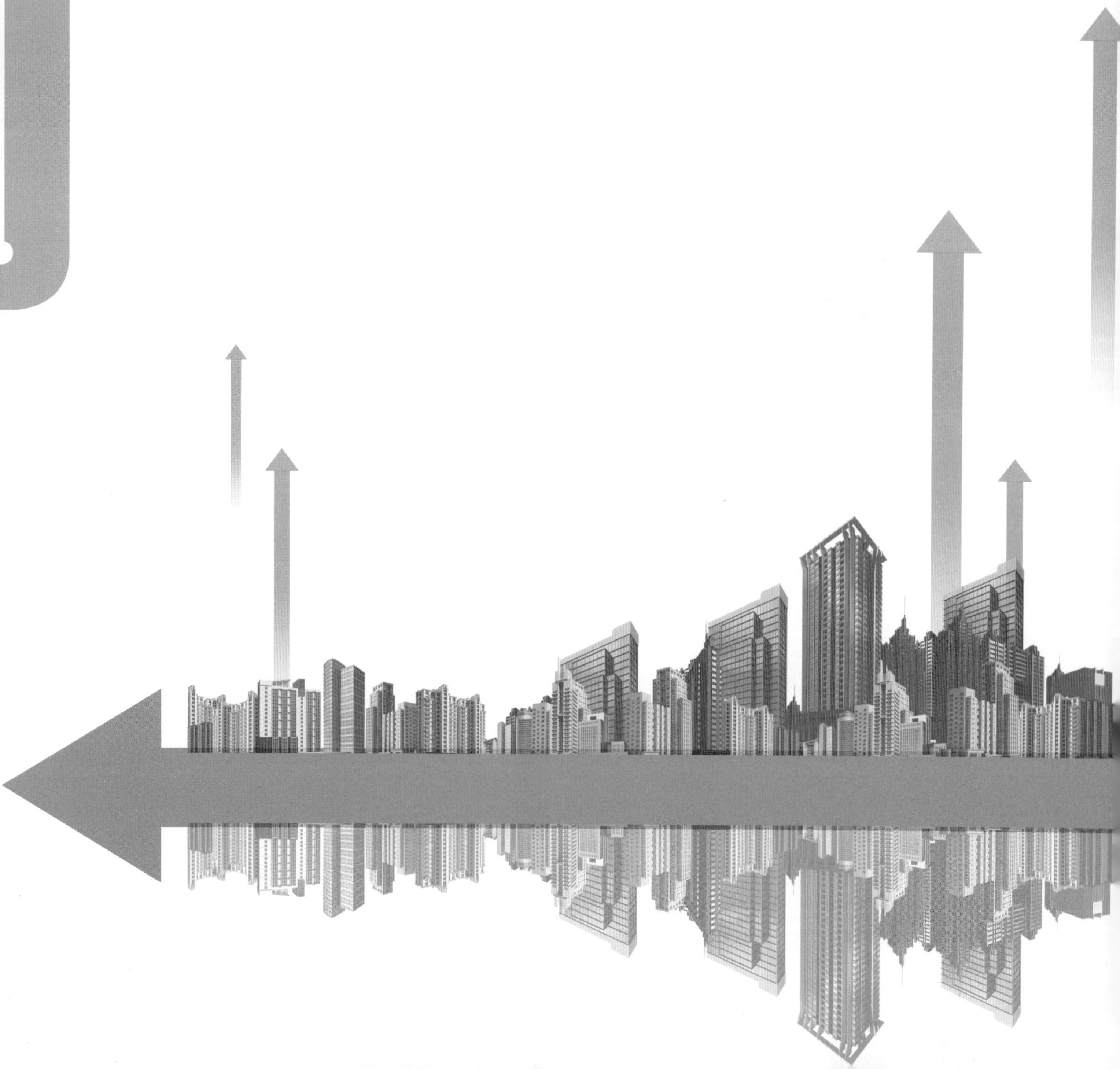

UNIT 03

# Claim Letter & Adjustment Letter

(배상요청 및 중재편지)

## 어휘 학습

| | |
|---|---|
| claim | v. 요구하다, 주장하다 n. 항의, 배상요구 |
| adjustment | n. 조정, 조절, 정리, 중재 |
| department stores | n. 백화점, 매장비품 |
| accounts receivable | n. 외상매출금, 받아야 할 금액 |
| accounts payable | n. 외상매입금, 지불해야 할 금액 |
| records | n. 기록, 이력 |
| delete | v. 지우다, 소거하다, 삭제하다 |
| statement | n. ①명세서, 신고 ②발표, 진술 |
| consideration | n. 고려, 대가 |
| matter | n. 물질 문제, 사건 |
| damaged | a. 손상된, 손해를 입은 |
| original | a. 본래의, 고유의, 원래의 |
| sales slip | n. 매상전표 (cf. pay slip 급여 명세표) |
| signature | n. 서명 |
| computerized | a. 컴퓨터 화된 |

- code　n. 법전, 암호, 약호
- fraudulent　a. 사기의, 부정한, 속이는 (fraud n. 사기, 사기꾼)
- signator　a. 서명자
- culprit　n. 죄인, 피의자
- apprehend　v. ①(격식)~을 체포하다 (= arrest) ②염려하다 ③이해하다
- legitimately　ad. 바르게, 합법적으로 (legitimate a. 합법의)
- assume　v. 취하다, 떠맡다, 추정하다
- entire　a. 전체의, 온전한
- appliances　n. 기구, 장치, 수단
  kitchen appliances 주방용품 / electrical appliances 전기기구
- flaw　n. 결점, 흠, 결함
- take responsibility　(숙어) 책임을 지다. (= be responsible for~)
- assure　v. 보증하다. 확실하게 하다.
- recur　v. 되돌아가다, 재발하다
- make up　n. 구성, 구조 마무리 v.보상하다
- refund　n. 반환, 환불
- crate　n.나무상자 v. 나무상자에 넣다
- rough　a. 거친, 대강의, 미완성의
- previous　a. 이전의, 사전의
- consequently　a. 결과로서 일어난
- duplicate　a. 이중의, 중복의, 복제의 v. 사본을 만들다, 복제하다
- patronage　n. 단골 거래, 애용
- disregard　v. 무시하다, 주의하지 않다

## Claim Letter A

**RAYMOND L. LOWISS**
April Court, Unit 4-E
1534 S. Havenview Street
Ponca, NB 43217

January 12, 2007

Freman-Stokes Department Stores
Accounts Receivable Department
5678 Center Street
Omaha, NB 43201

Dear Sirs :

In regard to my credit account statement dated December 31, please note that an item has been billed to me in error.

The leather jacket listed on page 1 was not purchased by me. Please check your records and delete this item from my account.

Enclosed is my check for $173.50, which should cover the remaining items on the statement.

Thank you for your consideration in this matter.

Sincerely yours,

Raymond L. Lowiss

## 적절한 답을 고르시오.

1. Who wrote the claim letter?

ⓐ Mr. Lowiss

ⓑ Freman–Stokes Department Stores

2. Who will write the adjustment letter?

ⓐ a clerk in the A/R Dept.

ⓑ a clerk in the Personnel Dept.

3. What is the problem?

ⓐ There was an error in the bill.

ⓑ The leather jacket was damaged.

4. When was the credit account statement dated?

ⓐ January 12

ⓑ December 31

5. How much was the original bill?

ⓐ $173.50

ⓑ more than $173.50

ⓒ less than $173.50

## Adjustment to Claim Letter A

FREMAN-STOKES
5678 Center Street
Omaha, NB 43201
413/555-0002

January 17, 2007

Raymond L. Lowiss
April Court, Unit 4-E
1534 S. Havenview Street
Ponca, NB 43217

RE : Account #1-473-00296

Dear Mr. Lowiss:

Thank you for your letter and payment dated January 12.

We have investigated the matter of the leather jacket and find that, according
to our records, it was purchased on your credit card. A copy of the sales slip, including the signature of the purchaser and the computerized credit card code, is enclosed.

If this item has been purchased fraudulently by someone other than an authorized signator, please contact our office immediately, and we will assist you in taking the necessary legal steps to apprehend the culprit.

If we do not hear from you within 30 days, we will assume that the item was purchased legitimately, and the purchase amount will remain on your bill.

We appreciate your patronage. If you have any questions, please do not hesitate to call me personally at the number shown above.

Very truly yours,

Kathy Chang

Enclosure

## 1. 배상 요구와 중재(Claim & Adjustment Letter)

넓은 의미의 배상요구(claim)는 손해 배상을 구체적으로 요구하는 적극적인 경우는 물론이고 불평(complaint)이나 경고(warning) 등도 포함될 뿐 아니라 상대방에게 불만을 느끼고 있으나 외부로 표현하지 않는 잠재 불만도 포함된다. 그러나 흔히 클레임이라고 하는 것은 무역 거래에 있어서 계약 당사자 일방의 계약 위반으로 인하여 손해를 입거나 불만을 가진 측이 손해를 입힌 측에 대하여 물품이나 금전 등의 구체적인 손해 배상을 요구하는 적극적인 것을 말한다.
클레임이 발생한 경우에는 원인에 따라 청구 내용을 확정하여 청구의 취지, 청구 이유, 손해 산출 명세, 주장의 근거 등 모든 사항을 자세히 기술하여야 한다.

### ▶ 배상 요구 편지

제품이나 서비스에 문제가 있을 경우, 개인 또는 회사를 대상으로 그 내용을 알리는 편지이다. 작성할 때 다음의 사항에 유의한다.

① 문제의 책임이 확실하게 상대에게 있는 가를 확인한다.
예를 들어, 제품이 파손된 경우 포장 상태를 점검한다. 그리고 기록 사항-선적 기록, 하적 서류(B/L), 수화물 전표, 날짜, 번호, 이름, 배달일 선적일, 주문 번호, 등등-여타의 도움이 될 사항을 검토하여 확인한다.
더 많은 정보를 찾을수록, 배상 문제를 해결하는 것이 수월해진다.

② 편지를 보낼 때에는 가능한 회사명이 아닌 개인의 이름 앞으로 작성하고 편지의 성격상 감정적으로 치우치기 쉬우므로 그러한 점에 대해 주의한다. 감정적인 항의만 하고 해당 문제에 대한 대책을 제시하지 않으면 오히려 역효과를 초래할 수도 있다. 그러나 너무 정중할 필요는 없다. 어디까지나 논리적으로 이쪽의 의향을 당당하게 표현하여 책임 소재를 명확히 하고 대책을 요구하는 것이 좋다.

▶ 배상 요구 편지의 구조

**1. 머리말은 문제를 언급하고, 가능한 한 자세한 정보를 제시한다.**

Ex In regard to my credit account statement dated December 31, please note that an item has been billed to me in error.

↓

**2. 본문은 편지를 쓰는 이유, 자신이 겪은 불이익 등등 이쪽의 곤란한 상황이 상대에게 충분히 전달될 수 있도록 설득력 있고 객관적인 문장으로 쓴다.**

Ex The leather jacket listed on page 1 was not purchased by me. Please check your records and delete this item from my account.

↓

**3. 문제 해결을 위한 요구 사항을 밝힌다. 불만을 해소하기 위해 합리적인 요구를 해야 하며, 그 대책을 제시한다.**

Ex Enclosed is my check for $173.50, which should cover the remaining items on the statement.

↓

**4. 맺음말은 상대방이 문제를 적절하게 처리해 줄 것이라는 신뢰를 보여준다.**

Ex Thank you for your consideration in this matter.

## 2. 불만 편지(혹은 배상 요구)에 대한 중재(Adjustment to Claim Letter)

무엇보다도 불만의 편지는 신속히 답해 주어야 한다. 불만 또는 조정의 조치가 지연된다면, 발신자에게 편지의 수신과 문제의 해결 노력에 대해 통보해야 한다. 신속하지 못한 태도는 이미 제품이나 서비스에 불만이 있는 고객의 실망을 가중시킬 뿐이다.

불만 편지는 귀하가 고객의 요구 - 환불, 재선적(교환), 혹은 여타의 요구 - 에 동의한다면, 해결은 보다 쉬워질 것이다.

편지의 서두는 자세한 사항을 상술해야 한다. 예를 들면, 불만사항의 발생이유를 간략히 설명하고 보상(배상)이 어떻게 이루어질지, 지불액은 은행 계좌에 입금될 것인지, 혹은 현금으로 지불될 것인지 등을 제시한다. 진심어린 사과와 더불어, 회사가 그러한 일이 다시는 발생하지 않도록 노력하겠다는 약속을 포함하는 것도 바람직하다.

아무런 준비가 없이 조정 편지를 쓰는 것은 위험한 일이다. 일단 문제가 발생하였다면, 문제를 해결하고 사과하는 편지는 매우 신중하게 해야 한다.

맺음말은 정중하며, 계속적인 거래를 당부하는 말이 포함되는 것이 좋다.

## Claim Letter B

FREMAN-STOKES
5678 Center Street
Omaha, NB 43201
413/555-0002

January 12, 2007

AQR Electronics
1234 South Main Street
Quincy, IL 30200

RE : Our PO #23-401, dated 12/01/90

Dear Sirs:

The above order, which you shipped on January 1, has been received damaged. We are, therefore, returning the entire shipment to you with the request that you will reship immediately, as we are in urgent need of these goods.

We appreciate the courteous, efficient service you have given us over the years, and we look forward to your prompt action in this matter.

Yours truly,

George Randall
Supervisor, Appliances Dept.

GR: al
cc : S. Hambull, Receiving
A. Rudolph, Accounts Payable

## 적절한 답을 고르시오.

**1.** The merchandise has been arrived in good condition.

ⓐ Yes

ⓑ No

**2.** The buyer requested a refund and returned the goods.

ⓐ Yes

ⓑ No

**3.** This is the first order between George and Freeman-Stokes.

ⓐ Yes

ⓑ No

**4.** Upon receipt of this letter, what should the vendor do first?

ⓐ Apologize to the customer

ⓑ Back-order a new merchandise

## Adjustment to Claim Letter B

AQR ELECTRONICS

1234 South Main Street
Quincy, IL 30200
313/555-6347

January 16, 2007

Freman-Stokes Department Stores
Appliances Department
5678 Center Street
Omaha, NB 43201

ATTN: George Randall, Supervisor

Dear Mr. Randall:

We have received your letter of January 12, along with the damaged merchandise. Please accept our most sincere apologies.

We have investigated the matter and discovered a flaw in our packaging system, which we have now corrected. We take full responsibility and have taken steps to assure that the same problem does not recur.

We also have made a 10% adjustment on your invoice, to make up for the inconvenience, and we are reshipping by overnight express at no cost to you.

We appreciate your patronage and look forward to serving your needs for many more years.

Sincerely,

## 적절한 답을 고르시오.

**1.** AQR 전자에서는 항의 편지와 함께 손상된 물품도 받았다.

ⓐ Yes

ⓑ No

**2.** 물품이 손상된 상태로 배달된 원인은 무엇인가?

ⓐ 운송과정에서 잘못됨.

ⓑ 이 회사의 포장시스템에 문제가 있었음.

**3.** 이번 실수에 대해 어떤 조치를 취하고 고객에게 보상을 하였는가?

ⓐ ______________________________

ⓑ ______________________________

ⓒ ______________________________

## Claim Letter C

**WILSON & COMPANY, Ltd.**

51 Wimbleton Road

Toronto, Ontario M4D 2V8 Canada

(416) 888-4444

FAX (416) 999-4443

May 18, 2007

Mr. Roland Fischer, Manager
New Tech Furniture
454 Liberty Road
Philadelphia, Pennsylvania 19148

Dear Mr. Fischer:

On May 1, I ordered an Executive desk Model No. ED418. On May 17, I received the furniture and found it damaged.

I am returning it to you today.

Please send me the new one as soon as possible. Also please correct my account -- No. 894-WC. The invoice was for five hundred and thirty-two dollars ($532.00); it should be five hundred and twelve dollars ($512.00).

Thank you for your assistance.

Cordially yours,

*David Lee*
David Lee

적절한 답을 고르시오.

1. David wrote this letter to place an order.

ⓐ Yes ⓑ No

2. Mr. Lee is returning the furniture to New Tech Furniture.

ⓐ Yes ⓑ No

3. Mr. Lee wants a refund.

ⓐ Yes ⓑ No

4. Did Mr. Lee enclose a check?

ⓐ Yes ⓑ No

5. Has Mr. Lee been billed?

ⓐ Yes ⓑ No

6. The model number was ED418.

ⓐ Yes ⓑ No

7. There was an error on the invoice.

ⓐ Yes ⓑ No

## Adjustment to Claim Letter C

Claim Letter C에 대한 Adjustment Letter를 보기에서 적절한 단어를 넣어 완성하시오.

> convenience, careful, carefully, shipping, handling, inconvenienced, shipped, damage, consequently, happy, apologize, in, duplicate, for, revised, regard, disregard, May 18, May 1

**New Tech Furniture**

454 Liberty Road

Philadelphia, Pennsylvania 19148

May 20, 2007

Mr. David Lee
Wilson & Company, Ltd.
51 Wimbleton Road
Toronto, Ontario M4D 2V8 Canada

Dear Mr. Lee:

Thank you very much for your letter of __________.

I am sorry you have been ________ by the ________ that was done to the furniture we ________ to you. The furniture was ________ crated; ________ it must have received rough ________ by the trucker. Also we sincerely ________ for the error ________ our invoice.

A ________ shipment is on its way to you and should arrive soon. We enclosed a ________ invoice of five hundred and twelve dollars (US$512.00). Please ________ the previous one.

Yours truly,
Roland Fisher
Manager

Enclosure

## 문법 따라하기 : 수동태

비즈니스 서신에서는 종종 능동태를 대신하여 수동태가 쓰인다. 수동태는 더 전문적이고, 덜 공격적인 느낌을 준다.

아래의 수동태와 능동태 문장의 예를 살펴보자. 능동태 문장에서는 주어가 목적어에 대하여 어떤 행동(동사)을 하지만, 수동태에서는 주어가 어떤 사람/사물에 의해 어떤 행동(동사)을 받거나 당한다. 즉, 능동태의 주어는 동작의 주체가 되지만, 수동태에서의 주어는 동작의 객체가 된다.

예시 1

능동태 : Vice President Atkins taught me to call you.

수동태 : I was taught to call you by Vice President Atkins.

예시 2

능동태 : Your partner at Newton Inc. gave me your name.

수동태 : Your name was given to me by your partner at Newton Inc.

### 다음의 능동태 문장을 수동태로 바꾸시오.

1. Our office does not sell the item.

______________________________

2. She will not need this product until June.

______________________________

3. Your assistant made a mistake in filling my order.

______________________________

4. The marketing department sends a magazine each month.

5. His boss often donates money to charity.

6. I have delivered the package as requested.

7. They have not received your letter yet.

8. He will order extra stock for the holiday season.

9. You did not answer my question.

10. One of your associates referred us to you.

## 문법 따라잡기 : 사역동사 have

have가 사역동사로 사용되면 다음의 예문처럼 [누구가/무엇이] [...을 하게 하다/시키다]는 의미를 갖는다.

예문 1

The president had her go to the convention in his place.
(사장님은 그를 대신하여 그녀가 그 전시회에 가도록 했다.)

예문 2

Please have your secretary call me.
(귀하의 비서가 저에게 전화하도록 해 주십시오.)

have 다음에 나온 동사(go, call)는 'to 부정사'대신 쓰인 원형 부정사이다. have 대신에 유사한 의미로 사용될 수 있는 동사들로는 ask, get, tell, instruct, require, request 등이 있는데 이 동사들은 원형 부정사 대신에 'to 부정사'를 취한다.

예문 1

The President told her to go to the convention in his place.
(사장님은 그를 대신하여 그녀가 그 전시회에 가라고 말했다.)

예문 2

Please instruct your secretary to call me.
(귀하의 비서가 저에게 전화하도록 지시하십시오.)

have 동사가 '...가/이 ...을 하게 하다/시키다'의 의미로 쓰였을 때에는 다음에 원형 부정사가 나오는 것을 명심하고 다음의 문장들을 HAVE를 사용하여 바꿔 쓰시오.

1. We will tell the union to meet with us as soon as possible.

2. The company require all construction workers to wear helmets.

________________________________________________

3. Sunflower Corporation asks potential suppliers to submit open bids.

________________________________________________

4. Your colleague asked me to send you the enclosed item.

________________________________________________

5. The director instructed the all staffs to organize the files.

________________________________________________

6. Please don't get the PR department to publish the new brochure until this week.

________________________________________________

7. Could you please ask Ms. Lee to contact Mr. Park.

________________________________________________

8. Please get your secretary to attend next month's annual meeting.

________________________________________________

9. We requested our financial department to forward the stocks to shareholders.

________________________________________________

10. My office does not require secretaries to work overtime.

________________________________________________

## Claim Letter D

# Future Manufacturing Co. Ltd

1234 Golf Avenue

Glenview, IL 91114

(405) 624-2614

FAX (405) 624-2616

April 15, 2007

Mr. John Hartford, Manager
Fossy Leather Company
3366 Chestnut Street
Lafayette, CA 17357

Dear Mr. Hartford :

On April 10, I ordered two bags numbers FL-331 and FL-336 each. However, I received two bags of number FL-334 and FL-335 on April 14.

Since these bags are not the ones I requested, I am returning--under separate cover--the two bags.

Would you please send me the two bags I originally ordered. Also please correct my account--No. 3372. The invoice was for four hundred thirty-six dollars and ninety-nine cents($436.99), but it should be for three hundred thirty-six dollars and ninety-nine cents($336.99).

Thank you in advance very much for your cooperation.

Cordially yours,

*Linda Choi*

Linda Choi

## Adjustment to Claim Letter D

Claim Letter D에 대한 Adjustment Letter

**Fossy Leather Company**

3366 Chestnut Street

Lafayette, CA 17357

(316) 555-2345 · FAX (316) 555-2346

April 18, 2007

Linda Choi
Future Manufacturing Co. Ltd
1234 Golf Avenue
Glenview, IL 91114

Dear Ms. Choi :

Thank you very much for your letter which we received on April 17.
We sincerely apologize for the  error.

As you requested, two bags of number FL-331 and FL-336--will be sent by overnight mail. You will receive it tomorrow. Upon receipt of new bags, please return the previous package--bags of FL-334 and FL-335-- and the invoice of $436.99 by mail. A new invoice (No. 9742) for $336.99 is enclosed.

Once again, we regret the error and apologize for any inconvenience. If we can be of any further service to you, please let me know.

Sincerely yours,

*John Hortford*
Supply Manager

Enclosure : Invoice No. 9742

## Claim Letter E

다음 Claim Letter E를 번역하시오.

HK Trading Company ltd.

1127 Harverview Avenue

Fairfax, VA 22210

(800) 334-2564

FAX (800) 334-2566

April 20, 2007

Mr, John Howard, Manager
European Leather Corp.
3456 Chestnut Rd.
West Lafayette, IN 47906

Dear Mr. Howard :

This letter is in reference to the order placed by us on March 16, 2007.

In this order, two bags were requested ; Item No. LB-3115 and LB-3226. However, on April 20, we received two(2) bags of item No. LB-3116 instead.

Since these bags are not the ones we requested, I am returning them to you under separate cover along with the invoice for four hundred dollars and ninety-nine cents($400.99).

Would you please ship, as soon as possible, the two(2) bags that we originally ordered--Item No. LB-3115 and LB-3226--along with a corrected invoice for three hundred-seven dollars and eighty-five cents($307.85). We would appreciate it if you would also reflect these changes on our account--No. 246 - HKT.

Thank you very much for your assistance.

Cordially yours,
*Terresa Kim*
Terresa Kim

번역

## Adjustment Letter E

다음의 Adjustment Letter E를 번역하시오.

**European Leather Corp.**

3456 Chestnut Rd.
West Lafayette, IN 47906
(765) 555-3300 · FAX (765) 555-3301

April 26, 2007

Terresa Kim
HK Trading Company Ltd.
1127 Harverview Avenue
Fairfax, VA 22210

Dear Ms. Kim :

Thank you very much for your letter which we received April 23 concerning our error in the completion of your order. We apologize for any inconvenience we may have caused you.

The two(2) bags which you originally requested--No. LB-3115 and LB-3226 --are being sent to you by overnight mail. You should receive them tomorrow. As you requested, we have enclosed a new invoice(No.8331) for $307.85.

If there are further problems, or if the bags do not arrive tomorrow as expected, please do not hesitate to contact me through fax or phone number listed above.

Once again, we apologize for the error in our shipment and any inconvenience this error may have caused. If I can be of any other service to you, please let me know.

Sincerely yours,

*John Howard*

John Howard
Manager

Enclosure : Invoice No. 8331

번역

UNIT

# 04

# Collection Letters & Reply

(수금 편지와 회신)

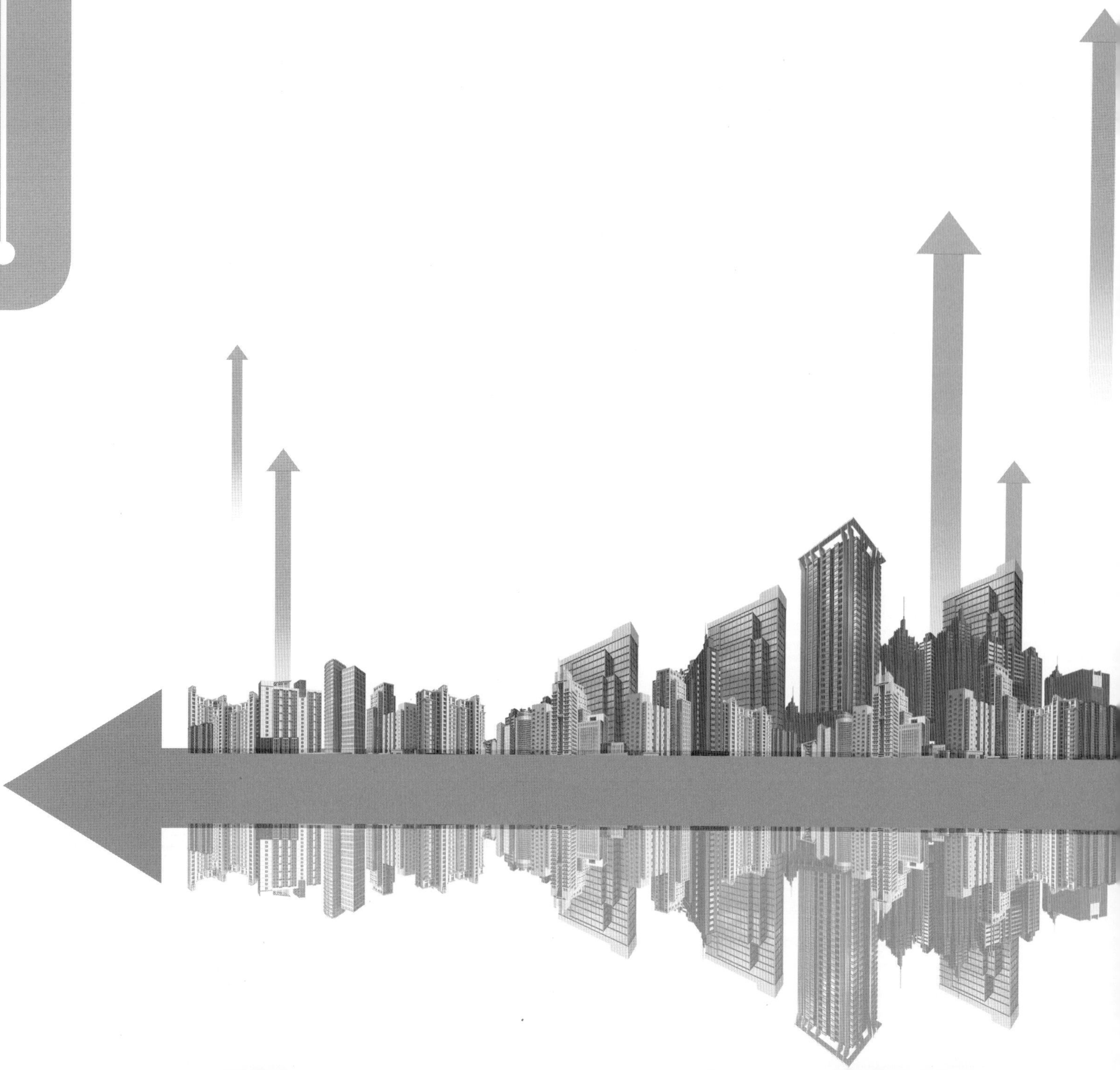

UNIT 04

# Collection Letters & Reply
(수금 편지와 회신)

## 어휘 학습

| | |
|---|---|
| • merchandise | n. 상품, 재고품 v. 장사하다 |
| • credit department | n. 신용거래부 |
| • remind | v. 생각나게 하다, 상기시키다, 일깨우다 |
| • overlook | v. 간과하다, 못 보고 지나치다 |
| • due to | 〈숙어〉 ~에 기인하는, ~때문에 |
| • cause | n. 원인, 이유 |
| • money order | 우편환, 송금수표, 자기앞 수표(소액에 쓰임) |
| • stimulate | v. 자극하다, 격려하다 |
| • definite | a. 확정된 (definitely ad. 완전히, 분명히) |
| • poise | n. 몸가짐, 평정, 평형, 침착, 냉정<br>v. 균형을 유지하다 |
| • tact | n. 재치, 기지, 임기응변의 재주 |
| • self-reliance | n. 자기의존, 자기신뢰 |
| • economical | a. 경제적인 |
| • upkeep | n. 유지, 보존 |

| | |
|---|---|
| checkbook | n. 수표장 |
| checkbook balance | 수표책 결산 잔고 |
| enumerate | v. 열거하다 (enumeration n. 열거, 목록) |
| deduct | v. 공제하다 (유. subtract, take away) |
| monotonous | a. 단조로운 |
| tiresome | a. 귀찮은, 성가신 |
| constant | a. 불변의, 일정한 (constantly ad. 계속, 끊임없이) |
| forget | v. 잊다, 망각하다 (과거분사 forgotton) |
| enthusiastically | ad. 열광적으로 |
| wander | v. 돌아다니다, 걸어다니다 |
| manuscript | n. 원고 |
| merit | n. 장점 |
| statement | n. 말함, 주제의 표현 |
| merely | ad. 단지, 다만 (only 보다 더 격식) |
| patient | a. 인내심 있는 |
| misfile | v. 잘못 철하다(정리하다) |
| patience | n. 인내, 참을성 |
| deadline | n. 최종 기한 |
| extend | v. 연기하다 |
| investigation | n. 조사, 연구 |
| best-run | a. 가장 잘 운영되는 |
| overdue | a. 연체된, 지급 기한이 지난 |
| recourse | n. 의지, 의뢰 |
| bookkeeper | n. 회계장부 기입자 |

## Collection Letter

**COCKATOO**

4753 Grand Street

Boston, Mass 01234

(312) 555-4567

May 12, 2008

Mr. James Smith

Vice President

XYZ Company

85 Aldeberry CT

Edison, NJ 09910

Dear Mr. Smith:

The cost of the merchandise you purchased from us several months ago was $25. However, we have not yet received your payment for this merchandise.

Won't you please send us your check for $25 without delay. A stamped, self-addressed envelope is enclosed for your convenience.

Sincerely yours,

Jean Marks

Credit Department

Enclosure

## 적절한 답을 고르시오.

1. $25를 지불해야 하는 사람은?

ⓐ Mr. Smith

ⓑ Mr. Marks

2. 이 수금편지를 쓴 사람은?

ⓐ Mr. Smith

ⓑ Mr. Marks

3. 지불 마감기한은 언제인가?

ⓐ within 1 month

ⓑ immediately

4. 이 편지를 쓴 목적은 무엇인가?

ⓐ to remind Mr. Smith of his overdue payment

ⓑ to say thank you for purchasing the merchandise

## Reply to a Collection Letter

**XYZ COMPANY**

85 Aldeberry CT
Edison, NJ 09910

May 14, 2008

Mr. Jean Marks
COCKATOO
4753 Grand Street
Boston, Mass 01234

Dear Mr. Marks:

Thank you very much for your letter of May 12 reminding me of my overdue payment.

I have just overlooked to pay it due to my busy schedule. A check for $25 is enclosed. Please accept my sincere apology for the inconvenience I may cause you.

Cordially yours,

James Smith
Vice President
XYZ Company

Enclosure

## 적절한 답을 고르시오.

1. 이 편지를 작성한 목적은 무엇인가?

ⓐ to pay the overdue bill

ⓑ to remind the overdue account

2. 늦은 지불에 대해서 사과하고 있는 사람은 누구인가?

ⓐ Mr. Smith

ⓑ Mr. Marks

3. 밑줄친 overlooked란 단어를 대체할 수 있는 단어는?

ⓐ forgot

ⓑ looked

ⓒ reminded

ⓓ saw

4. 이 편지에 동봉된 것은?

ⓐ a bill

ⓑ a check

ⓒ cash

ⓓ a money order

## Collection Letter의 작성 방법

'수금편지'는 지불 기한이 지났음에도 수금이 지연될 때 상대방에게 지불에 대한 내용을 상기시켜 주기 위해 작성한다.

다소 부정적인 내용이므로 고객의 기분이 상하지 않도록 정중하고 공손한 태도를 유지하는 것이 중요하다.

**1. 어떤 수금 건으로 편지를 보내는지 밝힌다.**

Ex The cost of the merchandise you purchased from us several months ago was only $25.

⬇

**2. 아직 수금되지 못했음을 알린다.**

Ex We have not yet received your payment for this merchandise.

⬇

**3. 기한을 명시한다.**

Ex Won't you please send us your check for $25 without delay.

OR

Would you please send us your check for $25 by May 25, 2008.

⬇

**4. 추가적인 정보를 제시한다.**

Ex A stamped, self-addressed envelope is enclosed for your convenience.

## Collection Letter에 대한 회신 작성방법

**1. 연체 사실을 알려준 것에 대해 감사한다.**

Ex Thank you very much for your letter of May 12 reminding me of my overdue payment.

**2. 지불기한을 넘긴 이유(사정)를 설명한다.**

Ex I have just overlooked to pay it due to my busy schedule.

**3. 지불방법이나 기한을 알린다.**

Ex A check for $25 is enclosed.

OR

I will send a check for $25 by May 25, 2008.

**4. 불편을 초래한 것에 대해 정중히 사과한다.**

Ex Please accept my sincere apology for the inconvenience I may cause you.

## General Information

### 1. Collection Letter

거래할 때 구매대금을 추후에 지불하기로 하는 경우도 많다. 만일 약속된 기일 내에 이들 대금이 지불되지 않는다면, 종종 고객에게 지불을 요구하기 위해 편지를 보내게 된다.
일반적으로 최초의 편지는 일정한 시기에 외상의 지불이 체납되어 있는 경우에 쓰이게 되며, 두 번째는 그로부터 일정 시간이 더 지난 후에 보내고, 순차적으로 이어진다.

수금 편지의 목적 : ❶ 먼저 기일 지난 대금을 청구하는 것.
: ❷ 고객의 호감을 잃지 않는 것.

만일 회사가 연체된 대금을 성공적으로 징수한다면, 고객으로 하여금 회사와 거래를 끊지 않고 차후의 구매를 계속 하도록 하는 것이 좋다.
회사마다 수금 정책과 과정은 다소 차이가 있으나 만기가 지난 계산을 청산하기 위한 단계는 일반적으로 다음과 같다.

### 2. Collection Letter의 단계

❶ 최초의 통보 : 연체 대금 지불을 요구하는 최초의 통보는 대개 고객의 기억을 환기시키는 것이 목적이다. 이는 대개 간단하다. 고무인, 인쇄된 메모, 또는 스티커 정도면 가능하며, 굳이 편지일 필요는 없다. 컴퓨터시스템에는 고객에게 외상 대금 지불이 만기가 되었음을 알리는 글이 추가되도록 프로그램 되어 있다. 지불 의무가 잊혀진 상황이라고 전제하고, 기억을 환기시켜 주는 것이다. 이때 수금 편지의 작성은 때때로 고객의 기분을 상하게 할 수도 있다.

❷ 두 번째 통보 : 두 번째 편지는 연체의 이유를 묻는, 실제의 편지이다. 고객이 연체에 대한 합당한 이유를 가지고 있다고 생각한다. 따라서 편지는 도움을 제공하는 어조를 띄게 된다. 고객이 지불을 할 수 있도록 모든 편리한 방법이 강구된다. 회신 우편봉투를 동봉하던지 또는 고객에게 전화나 다른 통신 방법으로 연락을 요청하는 일 등이다.

❸ 최후 통보 : 이전의 편지가 아무런 효력을 발생하지 못할 경우, 최후의 편지는 "당장 지불하시오. 아니면 법적 조치를 취할 것입니다."가 된다. 이 단계에서는 좋은 감정을 유지하는 것은 더 이상 중요한 일이 되지 못한다. 고객과의 거래를 원하겠지만, 부채의 상환이 더욱 중

요하다. 물론 욕설이나 격앙된 표현은 피해야겠으나, 편지의 어조는 강경하고, 단호하고, 또 명료해야 한다. 마지막 편지는 부채의 청산을 위해 노력한 지금까지의 과정을 다시 설명하여야 한다. 그것은 연체로 인해 어떤 결과가 고객의 신용도에 발생할 것인가를 밝히고, 체납이 지속될 경우 귀하(사)가 취하게 될 조치를 정확히 언급하여야 한다.

## 문법 따라잡기 : 콜론(:)

콜론은 그 다음에 오는 내용에 주목해야 한다는 의미이다.

**1)** 비즈니스 서신에서 콜론은 서두 인사말 바로 뒤에 사용한다.

- Dear Ms. Taylor:
- Ladies and(&) Gentlemen:

**2)** 시간 표현에서 시(時)와 분(分) 사이에 찍는다.

- 5:15 p.m.

**3)** 리스트, 숫자목록을 소개하는 문장 뒤에 쓰인다. 즉, as follows, the following, this, those 등과 같은 구절 등이 주로 목록 앞에 쓰인다.

- To stimulate committee action, a group needs the following characteristics : a good leader, a definite goal, and interested committee members.
- The person who will be hired for the secretarial position must have the following personal characteristics:
  ① Poise
  ② Tact
  ③ Self-reliance

**4)** 목록이나 강조하고 싶은 문장 앞에 콜론을 찍는다.

- An important rule of grammar is this: A complete sentence must have a subject and a predicate.
- Receptionists' duties include these: filing, typing, and handling incoming calls.
- 참조 : Receptionists' duties include filing, typing, and handling incoming calls.

**5)** 문장의 마지막 단어가 3)번 목록의 단어/어구들 같이 목록이나 강조 문장을 바로 지칭하지 않을 경우에는 콜론 대신에 마침표를 사용한다.

- If you keep these suggestions in mind, you will be able to be very economical.
  ① Prepare and use shopping lists. ② Examine articles carefully before buying them.
  ③ Consider upkeep and repair costs of major items.

**6)** 숫자 목록 앞 문장이라도 길이가 길고 마지막 구나 절이 3)번 목록의 단어/어구들처럼 목록을 직접 지칭하지 않으면 콜론 대신에 마침표를 사용한다.

- Your bank statement may not agree with your checkbook balance for one of the following reasons, which we have enumerated for your convenience.
  ① A mistake in calculation.
  ② Failure to deduct service charges.
  ③ One or more outstanding checks.

## 문법 따라잡기 : 대쉬(–)

대쉬는 '잠깐 멈춤'을 뜻하는 구두점 중 하나이다. 대쉬는 문장의 초점을 갑자기 바꾸거나, 생략되어도 무방한 내용을 삽입할 때 사용한다.

콜론과 대쉬의 차이점은 다음과 같다.
콜론은 읽는 이에게 바로 다음에 중요한 내용이 나온다는 걸 알리기 위해 사용하며, 대쉬는 문장에 갑자기 삽입되어서 다음에 나오는 내용을 눈에 띄도록 한다.

**1)** 콜론, 새미콜론, 대쉬를 모두 쓸 수 있는 경우에는 강조의 효과를 최대화 하기 위해서는 대쉬를 쓴다.

- My top drawer contains stationery supplies; namely, letterheads, clips, stapler, and envelopes.
- 참조: My top drawer contains stationery supplies-letterheads, clips, stapler, and envelopes.

**2)** 특별히 강조하기 위해서 앞의 내용을 반복할 때 사용

- The monotonous checking operations, the tiresome copying and recopying, the constant addition of new material - all were forgotten when the finished report was so enthusiastically received.
- Thanks! I appreciated your informative letter - an extremely informative letter, indeed.

**3)** 문장의 마지막 구/절을 강조하고 싶을 때 사용한다.

- Lucy wandered into the store, glanced at an expensive purse - and bought it.

**4)** 특별히 강조하고 싶은 부분, 공격적으로 보일 수 있는 부분을 완화하고 곧 나올 내용에 대해 읽는 이의 주의를 환기시키기 위해 사용한다.

- Here's a brand new pair of argyle socks - hand-knit, too!
- The budget requires considerable revision - but we will discuss that tomorrow.
- We are returning your manuscript - even though we think it has a great deal of merit.

## <연습문제> 콜론(:)과 대쉬(–)

다음의 각 문장들은 콜론이나 대쉬를 사용할 필요가 있다. 괄호 안에 적절한 구두점을 넣으시오.

**1.** I think I know who made the following statement (          ) "Tomorrow is another day."

**2.** The equipments that we need for the camping trip (          ) blankets, lanterns, tent, stove and bug repellent (          ) were purchased a few days ago.

**3.** In Time (          ) or was it the Economist (          ) I read that there might be a huge strike.

**4.** The following statement was made in one of Shakespeare's famous tragedies (          ) "Neither a borrower nor a lender be...."

**5.** I merely said this (          ) "Please be courteous and polite."

6. My manager was quite angry when he made the following pronouncement (       ) "If you do not satisfy our clients, you will not be working here next year."

7. Glen's sister (       ) she's a flight attendant (       ) is going to talk to our class tomorrow.

8. His P.E. teacher (       ) I think his name is Mr. Kwon (       ) is getting married next month.

9. Your new suit is made of wool (       ) or is it cotton.

10. Three famous American authors (       ) Ernest Hemingway, John Updike, and Saul Bellow (       ) are on our reading list this year.

11. The devastating forest fire (       ) the one in Oregon (       ) destroyed more than 200 hectares of hardwood trees.

12. Christie's father is employed as a high-school principal in New York (       ) or is it LA?

13. My three dogs (       ) Fluffy, Francis, Loo (       ) are getting their distemper shots this afternoon.

14. Next week (       ) or maybe the week after (       ) I am going bowling with my friends.

15. His speech contained this statement (       ) "Our company is the best workplace in the world."

## 예제 1

아래의 보기에서 적절한 단어를 골라 다음 편지의 밑줄을 채우시오.

| slips, takes, bring, self-addressed, reminders, overlooked, check, overdue, remainders |
|---|

Dear Mr. Mack:

Have you just __________ sending us a payment on your __________ account, or did our previous __________ go astray?

In any event, won't you take a moment right now to put a ____________ for $200 in the mail, before the matter __________ your mind? A stamped, __________ envelope is enclosed.

Yours very truly,

Enclosure

## 예제 2

다음 편지에서 잘못된 부분을 찾아서 고치시오.

FREMAN-STOKES

5678 Center Street

Omaha, NB 43201

(413)/ 555-0002

January 12, 2007

Mr. Harold I. Jones
842 E. Fountain Place
Omaha, NB 43206

RE : Account No.BL34-0079

Dear Mr. Jones:

In reviewing your acount, we notece that we have not received a payment from you in over 60 days.

if you are experiencing finance or other difficulties at this time, prebenting you from make your regular payments, we feel that we can be fo help to you by working out a new payment plan that will suite your curent circumstences.

Please contact us by phone as soon as possible, so that we may discuss this sitaution with you. You has been a value customar far many years, and we want that good relationship to continue in the future.

Very sincerely yours,

Carmen Jacobs, Manager
Credit Dept.

CJ:aht

## 예제 3

다음 편지를 읽고 예제 2의 편지와 비교하여 차이점을 설명하시오.

FREMAN-STOKES
5678 Center Street
Omaha, NB 43201
413/555-0002

12 January, 2007

Mr. Ralph Quinton
755 E. Appleton Way
Omaha, NB 43209

RE : Account No.1-473-00266

Dear Mr. Quinton:

We regret that your account with us is now six months past due, no payment having been received since July 14, 2006.

We have made several attempts to contact you but have received no response to either our letters or our phone calls; therefore, we have no recourse but to turn this account over to our Legal Department for collection.

If you value your good credit, please contact us by phone to make arrangements for payment on your account. We hope to hear from you immediately.

Sincerely,

Carmen Jacobs, Manager
Credit Department

CJ: aht
cc: Legal Department/Collections

## 예제 4

다음 편지는 예제 2의 수금편지에 대한 회신이다. 아래의 보기에서 적절한 단어를 골라 다음 편지의 밑줄을 채우시오.

enclosed, for, took, to, patient, misfiled, patience, causing, on, returned, account, accountant, enclosure

**HAROLD I. JONES**

842 E.Fountain Place • Omaha, NB 43206 • 413/555-9072

January 30, 2007

Carmen Jacobs, Manager
Credit Department
Freman-Stokes Department Store
5678 Center Street
Omaha, NB 43201

Ref. : A/C NO. BL34-0079

Dear Ms. Jacobs:

As I mentioned in our phone conversation this morning, I have been out of the country ______ the last two months ______ business and ______ to find that the accounting firm that ______ care of my personal business had ______ some of the paperwork I had left with them, ______ missed payments on several of my accounts.

I now have a new ______, and we are working together to ______ straighten out the books. The check for $250 should bring my account with you up ______ date.

Thank you very much for your ______ and assistance.

Yours truly,

Harold I. Jones

Enclosure

## 예제 5

다음의 수금 편지를 해석하시오.

Dear Mrs. Cambridge:

We are particularly happy to acknowledge your letter of Friday, March 20, telling us that you will pay your bill no later than June 1 with three separate payments of $100 each.

If you are able to make these payments at monthly intervals as you suggest, this will be satisfactory to us. We will expect to receive your final payment on or before June 1.

We know you realize, Mrs. Cambridge, that your credit rating depends upon the way you pay your bills.  If for any reason you cannot make the payments as stated, please let us know promptly.

Very truly yours,

해석

## 예제 6

다음 편지는 예제 5의 수금편지에 대한 회신이다. 내용에 맞게 적절한 단어를 아래의 보기에서 찾아서 밑줄을 채우시오.

importance, possible, on time, therefore, make, deadline, final, look, extend, understand, pay, however

Dear Mr. Weber:

As you know, I made two payments of $100 each as I stated in my letter of March 20. Unfortunately, I now find it impossible to _______ the third payment _______ .

You can be sure that I understand the _______ of paying one's bills on time. Sometimes, _______ , one just cannot do what he knows to be best. This is my situation at this time.

While I cannot make the June 1 _______ , I will do everything _______ to make the third payment no later than July 1. I can only hope that you __________ my situation, Mr. Weber, and that you will _______ the time of my _______ payment.

Sincerely yours,

## 예제 7

다음의 수금과 관련된 편지들을 해석하시오.

Dear Mr. Wilson:

Thank you for your letter of November 18, telling us why you have not paid your bill. We are always happy to cooperate with a customer who cannot pay his bill when he tells us why he cannot do so.

We are, therefore, glad to give you the additional 30 days that you reguested.

Sincerely yours,

---

Dear Mr. Blair:

Thank you for writing us the reason why your November bill has not been paid.

We realize that there are occasions when the most successful business cannot pay its bills on time because of unforeseen circumstances. We have been in that position ourselves.

We shall be patient for another 30 days.

Very truly yours,

---

Gentlemen:

Please have your bookkeeper check our account again. We find upon investigation that we sent you a check for $150 on April 15, and our canceled check has been returned to us by the First National Bank.

I realize that mistakes can happen in the best-run organizations.

Very truly yours,

해석

해석

해석

UNIT 05

# Follow-up Letters & Congratulations Messages
(사후편지 및 축하메시지)

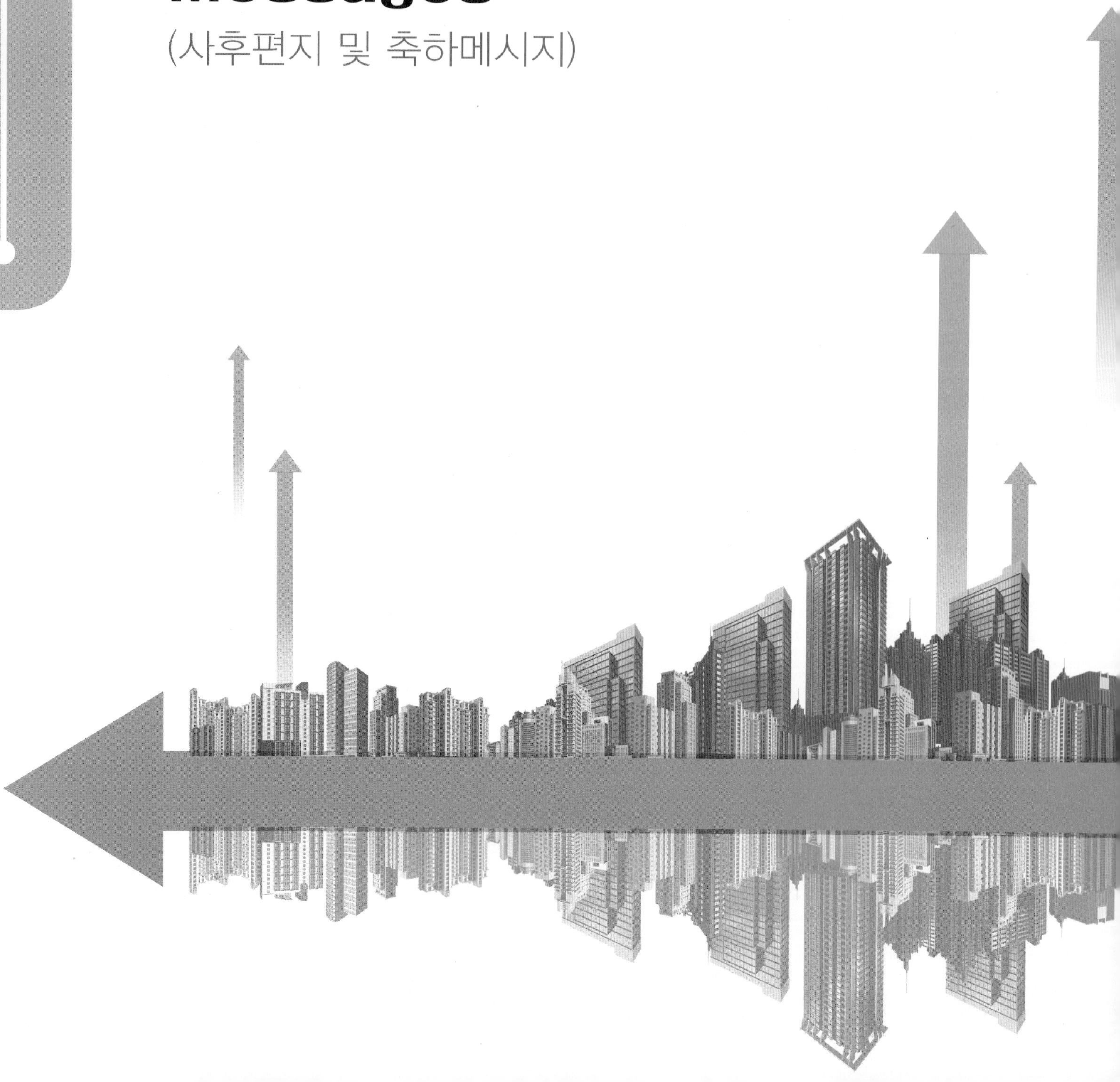

UNIT 05

# Follow-up Letters & Congratulations Messages

(사후편지 및 축하메시지)

## 어휘 학습

- fit — v. 맞다, 적합하다
- suggestions — n. 제안, 제언
- undecided — a. 아직 결정되지 않은, 미정인
- popular — a. 인기 있는, 평판이 좋은
- jot down — 〈숙어〉 적다, 필기하다 (= write down)
- wholesale — n. 도매, 대량 판매 (반. retail)
- ethics — n. 도덕 원리, 윤리 (유. morality)
- discriminating — a. 구별할 수 있는, 식별력이 있는 (discrimination n.편견, 차별, 구별, 식별)
- divulge — v. 누설하다, 폭로하다 (유. reveal)
- verite — n. 진실
- sketchy — a. 불완전한
- outline — v. ~의 윤곽을 그리다
- comply with — 〈숙어〉 응하다
- compliment — n. 경의
- civic — a. 시의, 도시의

| | |
|---|---|
| ● conflict | v. 충돌하다 / n. 투쟁, 싸움 |
| ● permit | v. 허용하다 |
| | (permission n.허가, 허용, 승인, 동의) |
| ● access | n. 입수, 이용, 접근 |
| ● upset | a. 혼란에 빠진, 엉망인 |
| ● doubt | v. 의심하다, 수상히 여기다 / n.의심, 의혹 |
| ● repairman | n. 수리공 |
| ● emergency | n. 비상사태, 위급 |
| ● unlikely | a. 가망 없는, 성공할 것 같지 않은 |
| ● be unlikely to~ | ~할 것 같지 않은 |
| ● especially | ad. 특히 |
| ● distribute | v. 유통시키다, 공급하다 |
| ● lawn | n. 잔디, 잔디밭 |
| ● deplete | v. 감소시키다, 다 써버리다, 고갈 시키다 |
| ● replenish | v. 보충하다, 공급하다 |
| ● vicinity | n. 근처, 부근 |
| ● afford | v. ~할 수 있다, ~할 여유가 있다 |
| ● unfair | a. 불공평한 |
| ● remittance | n. 송금 |
| ● preceding | a. 바로 앞의, 앞선 |
| ● retain | v. 계속 유지하다, 간직하다 |
| ● complimentary | a. 칭찬하는 |
| ● customary | a. 습관적인, 통례의 |
| ● state | v. 진술하다, 확언하다 |
| ● specifically | ad. 명확하게, 특히 |
| ● be accompanied with | 〈숙어〉 ~을 동반하다 |
| ● deserving | a. ~할 가치 있는 |
| ● tireless | a. 꾸준한, 부단한 |
| ● stuck | a. ~에 열중한 |
| ● stick to~ | (일, 공부 등) 끝까지 해내다, 전념하다 |

- accomplishment　n. 성취, 완성, 성과
- commend　v. 추천하다, 권하다
- pay off　성공하다, 기대했던 성과를 올리다 (= succeed)
- sympathy　n. 동정, 공감
- privilege　n. 특권, 영광
- sadden　v. ~을 슬프게 하다

상대방의 요청이나 부탁에 대해 거절하는 등 부정적인 답신을 할 때(Problem Letters)와 물품이나 현금, 수표 등을 송부할 때 (Transmittal Letters) 작성하는 Follow-up Letter들에 대해 알아볼 것이다. 또한 상대방의 생일, 승진, 영전, 개업 등을 축하하는 메시지 작성법과 함께 불행한 사고나 병 등 좋지 않은 일에 대한 위로의 메시지 작성법도 익히도록 한다.

## A. Problem Letters(문제 상황에서의 편지)

상대방의 요청에 대해 거절하는 편지는 승낙 편지보다 기술적이고 주의 깊은 접근법이 필요하다. 거절편지를 작성할 때에는 최대한 긍정적인 톤을 유지하면서 거절에 대한 대안을 제시하는 방법을 사용한다.

### 1. 불완전한 요청

비즈니스를 하다 보면 때로는 불명확 하거나 불완전한 요청을 받게 되는 경우가 흔하다. 그러한 경우에는 불완전한 정보를 확인해 줄 것을 요청하는 편지를 작성하게 된다. 그러나 상대방이 무심하거나 부주의하다고 책망하는 인상을 주지 않도록 조심해서 작성해야 한다.

예시 1-1

Gentlemen:

My friend and I are planning a vacation in Europe and would like to go with a tour group.

What are the rates?

Sincerely,
Mary Carter

위의 예시와 같은 경우에 몇 가지의 중요한 정보들이 빠져 있기 때문에 여행사 직원은 상대방이 만족할 만한 답신을 줄 수 없다. 성수기와 비수기에 따라 여행 경비가 다르므로 몇 월에 얼마동안 여행을 가기를 원하는지, 유럽의 어떤 국가들을 여행하고 싶은지에 대한 구체적인 정보가 없으면 적절한 답을 줄 수 없다. 따라서 다음과 같이 요령 있게 정보를 요청하는 회신 편지를 작성해야 한다.
상대방이 답신하기 쉽도록 편지를 작성해야 하며, 상대방의 잘못으로 충분한 정보를 제공하지 못했다는 인상을 주어서는 안 된다.

예시 1-2

Dear Mrs. Carter:

Thank you for writing to us for tour information for your vacation in Europe. We have a number of exciting and interesting tours that I feel sure will fit your plans.

So that we are sure to give you suggestions that exactly fit your interests, would you please answer several questions:

When do you plan to take your trip?
How long do you plan to be away?
What countries do you want to visit?

Since you may still be undecided about some of these answers, I am enclosing several brochures that will give you general information about some of our most popular tours. However, I can make many other suggestions when I know more about your plans and special interests.

In the margin of the enclosed copy of this letter, please jot down the answers to the above questions, and return it to me in the enclosed envelope. Just as soon as I receive your reply, I shall be happy to assist you in making your plans for your European vacation.

Sincerely yours,

## 2. 불합리한 요청

아래와 같이 때로는 불합리한 정보나 서비스를 요청하는 고객들도 있다.

예시 2-1

> Gentlemen:
>
> I am interested in buying one of your Electro Percolators. A friend told me that he could get me one wholesale.
>
> In order to know whether I'm getting a good price or not, I would appreciate having the wholesale price of the Electro Percolator.
>
> Very truly yours,

도매가(wholesale price)란 제조업체와 도매상과의 계약에 의한 가격이며, 기밀을 요하는 사항이므로 이러한 문의는 적절하지 않다. 그럼에도 불구하고, 상대방에게 '귀하의 요구는 부적절하다'라고 지적하기 보다는 우리 회사의 제품에 관심을 가져준 고객에게 감사를 표하면서 공식적인 구매 채널을 통해 구입할 것을 제안하는 방식으로 기술적으로 작성해야 한다.

예시 2-2

Dear Mr. Herbert:

Your interest in buying an Electro Percolator pleases us very much. You have selected the finest coffee maker available anywhere at any price.

The suggested retail price of the Electro is $29.95, and once you have seen the Percolator, you will agree that it is well worth every cent.
I wish I could tell you the wholesale price of the Electro Percolator, but standard business ethics require us to keep this information confidential between the manufacturer and the dealer. I know you will understand the reasons behind this policy.

Two stores in Salt Lake City carry Electro appliances-Goodson's and Star Appliances. These dealers are featuring Electro products this month. When you buy from an authorized dealer, you are sure of getting prompt service.

You will be delighted with the Electro Percolator. Once you have tried it, you will know why discriminating coffee lovers say, "I didn't know coffee could taste so good!"

Sincerely yours,

Exercise 다음 문장들은 불완전한 정보나 비합리적인 요청에 대해 회신하는 편지의 일부분이다. 각 문장이 상대방과 좋은 관계를 유지하기 위해 노력하는 문장의 예인지 아닌지 밝히시오.

1. We are sorry that we cannot give you the information you request. Frankly, we are surprised that you would ask us to divulge such personal confidences.

2. Thank you for your interest in purchasing verite carpeting in the Redrose pattern that you purchased from us 15 years ago. It was a particularly lovely pattern; unfortunately, however, the manufacturer discontinued it some time ago.

3. How do you expect us to figure out what you want when you always give such sketchy information?

4. As soon as you send us the details outlined below, we shall be glad to send you the information you request.

5. Since your request is unreasonable, we cannot possibly comply with it.

## 3. 초대에 대한 거절

회사와 비즈니스맨들은 때때로 외부행사 참여, 봉사활동, 강연, 시상식 등에 초청받기도 한다. 이러한 행사에 참여하는 것은 많은 의미가 있고 비즈니스에 도움이 되기도 하지만, 시간이나 재무적인 제약 때문에 이러한 초청을 거절할 수밖에 없는 경우도 있다.

초대에 거절하는 편지를 작성할 때는 다음의 순서를 따른다.

1. 초청에 대해 감사한다.
2. 거절할 수밖에 없는 타당한 이유를 제시한다.
3. (실제로 그렇게 할 의도가 있다면) 다음에 초대해 주면 응하겠다고 약속함으로써 가능성을 열어 둔다.

예시 3

Dear Mr. Ryder:

It was indeed a compliment to receive your letter asking me to serve on the Miami Committee for Civic Improvement. After reading the outline of the purpose of the committee, I feel certain that this group has great potential.

Unfortunately, Mr. Ryder, I shall not be able to accept your invitation to work with the committee, for the proposed meeting time - the third Wednesday of each month - conflicts with the staff meetings held in our organization.

If for any reason your meeting time is changed, and if you should still want me to serve, please let me know.

Cordially yours,

## 4. 정보요청을 거절할 때

모든 정보 요청에 응할 수는 없으며, 요구 자체가 불합리하거나 기밀을 지켜야 하는 정보일 때는 거절할 수밖에 없다.
정보 요청을 거절하는 편지는 대개 아래와 같이 간단명료하게 작성한다.

예시 4

Dear Mr. Barnes:

I am sorry that I am unable to send you information about Miss Sally Park. Personal data concerning our employees is considered highly confidential, and only our personnel department is permitted access to our files.

Very truly yours,

## 5. 주문이 지연될 때

고객은 언제나 좋은 품질의 제품과 서비스를 신속하게 제공받기를 기대한다. 하지만, 때로는 불가피하게도 주문이나 배송이 지연될 수 있고 이러한 경우에는 상황을 알리고 추후진행 일정을 알리는 편지를 신속하게 작성해야 한다.

이러한 편지는 다음의 순서를 따른다.

1. 고객에게 현재 시점에서 회사가 할 수 있는 것과 없는 것을 정확하게 구별하여 알린다.
2. 긍정적인 어조를 유지한다.
3. 고객이 회사나 회사의 제품에 대한 신뢰를 잃지 않도록 우호관계를 조성하는 표현을 삽입한다.
4. 향후에도 거래할 수 있도록 긍정적인 어조로 마무리한다.

예를 들면, 고객으로부터 신제품 건조기의 수리를 요청하는 편지가 왔다고 생각해 보자. 제품은 설치된 날 바로 고장이 났으며, 수리를 요청했으나 수리기사로부터 아무런 답이 없었다고 했을 때 고객에게 어떠한 회신을 작성해야 할까? 다음은 그러한 문제 상황에 적절하게 답하는 좋은 예이다.

예시 5

Dear Mrs. Donlevy:

We can naturally understand your concern that the dryer you purchased from us two weeks ago is still not in working order. Because we are just as upset about this as you, we are sending a replacement to you today.

Although there is little doubt that the dryer you have could be adjusted easily - the Whirler is an excellent machine - we are embarrassed to say that we just don't have a repairman available to call at your house. Normally we have two excellent repairmen who could fix your dryer; however, one is on vacation and the other was called to the West Coast on personal business. You can be sure that this is an emergency situation and is most unlikely to occur should you again need repair service.

The replacement dryer that we are sending today will be in working order tomorrow. Won't you stop in to see us again soon? We have a new-model Whirler air conditioner that is an especially fine product at an extremely low price.

Sincerely yours,

## 6. 주문에 대한 거절

대개의 경우 회사에서는 모든 주문을 기쁘게 받아야 하지만, 때로는 주문을 거절해야 할 때도 있다. 가장 흔한 경우는 개인고객이 도매상으로부터 물건을 사려고 할 때이며 이런 경우에는 가까운 소매점을 권해주어야 한다.

다음의 작성 순서를 따르는 것이 좋다.

1. 먼저 주문에 대해 감사한다.
2. 주문을 거절하는 이유를 밝힌다.
3. 제품을 어디서 구매할 수 있는지를 알려준다.

예시 6

Dear Mr. Thomson:

Thank you for your order for 150 square yards of Taupe Deepbrite carpeting, which you saw advertised in Homelite magazine. You have selected a pattern that you will enjoy in your new home, and Taupe Deepbrite will give you lasting beauty and long wear.

However, since we distribute our carpeting through retail stores only, we are not able to serve you directly. I am please to be able to refer you to Raymond's Home Furnishings at 7436 North State Street in Riverton. Raymond's carries our complete line of carpeting and will be happy to show you the pattern that you have selected.

Do stop in at Raymond's right away so that you can enjoy personal service in filling your carpeting needs.

Sincerely yours,

Exercise 다음 문장들은 주문이 지연되거나 주문을 거절하는 편지의 일부분이다. 상대방과 우호관계를 유지하기 위해 노력하는 의도가 보이는가에 대하여 답하시오.

1. This is the wrong time of the year for us to stock lawn furniture. Sorry we can't fill your order.

2. We very much appreciate your order for Snowflake sheets, and they will be mailed to you no later than the first of next month. You selected such a popular design that our stock is currently depleted.

3. Your order will be shipped just as soon as our stock is replenished.

4. Adjust-Rite lawn chairs will be in production again early in April. We hope you will agree to let us hold your order until the lawn chairs are ready for shipment to you.

5. You should realize that we are a wholesale store and cannot sell directly to you. There must be a retail store somewhere in your vicinity.

## 7. 불합리한 할인 요청을 거절할 때

때로는 고객이 할인율을 잘못 계산하거나, 적용할 수 없는 할인을 요구할 때가 있다. 이러한 경우에는 잘못된 금액을 수정하는 편지를 써야 한다. 다른 고객과의 형평성을 지키기 위해서 예외를 두어서는 안 되므로 회사는 다음의 방법 중 한 가지를 택해서 회신 편지를 작성해야 한다.

① 송금 받은 금액을 돌려보내고 정확한 금액을 입금해 줄 것을 다시 요구한다.
② 송금액을 받고 나서 차액의 입금을 요청한다.
③ 송금액을 받고 나서 고객의 다음 청구서 금액에 포함시킬 것을 알린다.

금액을 수정할 때는 상대방의 잘못을 지적하는 어조를 피하면서 수정해야 할 사항을 정확히 언급하는 요령이 필요하다.

예시 7

Dear Mr. Wheaton:
Thank you for your check for $2,450 in payment of your March invoice. We appreciate many opportunities you have given us to serve you.

We notice that, in the past, you have always paid your invoices within the discount period in order to take advantage of the saving. As you know, we can afford to give this discount because prompt payment enables us to make a similar saving on our purchases.

When a customer does not make payment within the discount period, we also do not make any saving. In this instance, you waited seventeen days before making payment. Of course, this is seven days beyond the maximum allowed.

Because you are a good customer and because this is the first time you have gone beyond the discount period, we should like to allow the discount. However, if we did so, we would be unfair to our customers who pay within the ten-day period. They would lose confidence in us, and so would you.

Therefore, Mr. Wheaton, will you please send us with your next remittance the $50 remaining on your account.

Very sincerely yours,

Exercise 다음 문장들은 거절편지의 일부분이다. 상대방과 우호관계를 유지하기 위해 노력하는 의도가 보이는가에 대하여 답하시오.

1. I'm sorry that I cannot accept your invitation to speak at your October meeting. I just don't have time for such things.

2. Thank you for giving me the opportunity to speak at you October meeting.

3. I am sorry that I cannot give you medical information about my patient, Mr. Ralph Jones.

4. Your request for information about our markup policy would require an unreasonable amount of work on the part of our staff.

5. In view of the preceding explanation, Mr. Reeves, we are crediting your account with the $250 and will expect the balance of $10 immediately.

## 예제 1

다음의 부정적 상황과 관련한 편지를 읽고 문법, 어법, 철자 등의 오류를 다음 표에 근거하여 찾아내서 정확한 표현으로 고치시오.(총 오류의 개수는 15개이다.)

| 오류의 종류 | 오류의 개수 |
|---|---|
| Capitalization | 2 |
| Punctuation | 1 |
| Grammar | 3 |
| Spelling | 7 |
| Pronoun | 2 |

Dear Mr. Field,

Thank you for ask Whitmere's to participate in your questionair concerning the number of employees that local forms hire yearly, their education background, his individual promotions, and other employment details. certainly the results of your study would be of interest to we, and we should like to participate.

because our staff is small, collecting the data would take more time then we can possibly afford. However, I shall be glad to met with you personally and to give you some estimated figures to answer the items on your questionnaire.

Cordially yours,

## 예제 2

다음의 두 편지를 읽고 해석한 뒤 차이점이 무엇인지 답하시오.

Dear Mr. Samuels:

Our order for lumber has not yet been received. We need this lumber immediately for a construction job on which we are working.

If you cannot deliver this lumber by September 5, please let us know so that we can place our order elsewhere.

Yours truly,

---

Dear Mr. Samuels:

Thank you for the special service you gave us on our order for lumber. It arrived on September 3, and we were able to use it on an important construction job.

You may be sure that we shall call on you again when we need lumber.

Yours very truly,

---

차이점

## B. Transmittal Letters(송금/송부 편지)

수표, 우편환, 또는 중요한 서류 등을 우편으로 송부할 때에는 이를 설명하는 편지와 함께 보내야 한다. Transmittal Letters는 무엇을 왜 보내는지 정확히 알림으로써 수신자가 보내는 사람의 의도를 정확히 파악할 수 있도록 한다. 또한 향후 증빙으로써 중요한 역할을 할 수도 있다.

Transmittal Letters는 다음의 구성요소를 갖춘다.

1. 무엇을 몇 개 보내는지 밝힌다.
2. 수표, 우편환 등을 보내는 것이라면 정확한 금액과 송금 목적을 명시한다.
3. 추후 follow-up이 필요하다면 무엇인지 밝힌다.

이러한 Transmittal Letters가 필요한 동봉물들은 주로 브로셔나 카달로그, 가격표, 수표, 보고서, 제안서, 계약서 등의 비즈니스 서류이다.

Transmittal Letters에 주로 사용되는 문구는 다음과 같다.

1. Enclosed are(is) ..................... (동봉물은 ... 입니다.)
2. We are enclosing ..................... (...을 동봉합니다.)
3. Attached please find .................... (...의 첨부물을 참조해 주십시오.)

예시 1

Dear Mr. McDade:

Enclosed are the original and one copy of the contract for your manuscript, *A Boy's Story of the War Between the States*. Please sign both copies, return the original to me, and retain the carbon.

The review by Oswald Carruthers of your manuscript was extremely complimentary. As you know, our target date for publication is October 15. I'll be in touch with you when editing begins.

Sincerely yours,

Enclosures

예시 2

Dear Mrs. Williams:

Enclosed is publication guideline for news releases for *The Daily Journal*. The parts that apply specifically to business news are highlighted for your convenience.

Mr. Adams asked me to also send you two sample business news releases that he thought might be helpful to you in preparing yours.

Sincerely,

Mary Carr
Assistant to Felix Adams

Enclosures

Exercise 다음의 Transmittal Letters에 대한 설명을 읽고 내용이 맞으면 T, 틀리면 F로 표시하시오.

1. The carbon copy provides a valuable reference because it shows what document the writer has sent and to whom the document was sent.

2. It is customary for the letter of transmittal to state specifically what, if anything, the reader is expected to do with the item being transmitted.

3. A check sent in payment of an account need not be accompanied with a letter because the recipient will know the purpose for which the check is intended.

## 예제 3-1

귀하는 Professional Golfer's Association에서 일하고 있다.
Ms. Kee Lewis가 오늘 귀하에게 전화를 해서 협회 가입 신청서를 보내 달라고 요청했으므로, 신청서 양식과 함께 협회에 대한 정보를 포함한 브로셔를 보내려고 한다. 아래의 커버레터 양식을 적절한 내용으로 채우시오.

| Professional Golfer's Association |
| --- |
| |

## 예제 3-2 : Double Check(재검토)

송부하기 전에 반드시 다시 한 번 내용을 검토하는 것이 바람직하다. 동봉물이 무엇인지 정확히 설명했는가? 동봉물을 보내는 이유를 설명했는가? 귀하가 작성한 예시 1의 편지를 다시 한 번 읽어보고 아래의 편지와 비교해 보시오.

Dear Ms. Lewis:

Enclosed is the application form for membership in the Professional Golfer's Association that you requested by phone this morning.

I've also enclosed a brochure that gives additional information about the Professional Golfer's Association. Please call me when I can be of further help.

Sincerely,

Bob Eakle

Assistant to Ms. Noggle

Enclosures

## 문법 따라잡기 : 새미콜론(;)

**1)** 복문에서 각각의 절이 접속사로 연결되지 않을 때, 각 절 사이에 새미콜론을 찍는다.

- The accident happened at three o'clock; it was not reported until five.
- Mr. Wilkins is a President of the association; Mrs. Wilkins is a Vice President; Dr. Willis is a Cheif Advisor.

**2)** 복문에서 두 번째 절이 아래와 같은 부사들로 시작되면 부사 앞에 새미콜론을 찍고 부사 뒤에는 콤마를 사용한다.

| accordingly | 따라서, 그러므로 | however | 그러나 |
|---|---|---|---|
| again | 다시, 또 | indeed | 참으로, 실로 |
| also | 또한, 역시 | moreover | 더욱이 |
| besides | 그 밖에, 게다가 | nevertheless | 그럼에도 불구하고 |
| consequently | 따라서 | otherwise | 만약 그렇지 않으면 |
| furthermore | 더군다나 | therefore | 따라서, 그 결과 |

- The accounting procedures have been revised; however, your work will remain unchanged.
- Mr. Ryan must complete a rush job this week; consequently, Ms. Dunkan will work with him for a few days.

**3)** 두 개의 절이 for example, for instance, namely, that is 와 같은 "예를 들면, 말하자면"이라는 의미의 연결어로 이어질 때, 연결어 앞에 새미콜론을, 뒤에는 콤마를 찍는다.

- The survey was very successful; that is, more than 70 percent of those receiving a questionnaire completed and returned it.
- When you transcribe the letter, don't forget to add reference initials; for example, KM/jh or KM:JH

**4)** 콤마가 여러 번 사용된 복문에서 각각의 절을 나눠줄 때에도 콤마를 사용하면 읽는 이에게 혼란을 줄 수 있으므로, 이런 경우에는 세미콜론을 사용한다. 이해가 잘 된다면 콤마만 사용해도 충분하다.

- We ordered staples, hanging files, and carbon paper; plain paper and pencils were sent instead.

- Ms. Yoon, secretary to Mr. Koh, bought the invitations, and her colleagues helped her prepare and mail them.

**5)** 콤마를 포함한 아이템이 여러개 있을 때는 각 아이템 다음에 새미콜론을 찍어서 의미의 혼동이 없도록 한다.

- Sales conferences will be held in Houston, Texas; Washington, D.C.; and Raleigh, North Carolina.

## 연습 문제 : 새미콜론(;)

다음 문장에서 새미콜론이 필요한 부분에 새미콜론을 삽입하고, 정확한 문장에는 C를 표시하시오.

1. No, I think the physics that is scheduled for Monday, the biology test is on Tuesday.

2. My laptop does not have enough memory, nevertheless I must continue using it until I have enough money to buy a more poweful one.

3. Laura is an excellent dancer, she is expecially good at folk dance.

4. The general manager the audit manager, and Hery Chan our accountant, are having an emergency meeting.

5. None of us knows how to play golf, however we are all eager to learn.

6. Listening classical music often, for example, consider listening Bach, Mozart, and Beethoven.

7. Let's get off the bus stop, I didn't bring my assignment.

8. Our senior almost lost his wallet on the subway, fortuately an honest person found it on the seat and returned it to him.

9. After we saw the musical, we had dinner in a famous chinese restaurant, but Susan, after eating her shark's fin.

10. David, Henry John, and Roland are all members of our fitness center.

11. I must study longer hours I'm falling behind in my studies.

12. Try eating foods that are less fattening, for instance, eat fruit for dessert instead of ice cream.

## C. Congratulations Message(축하 메시지)

축하 메시지는 상대방의 생일, 기념일, 결혼, 출산, 이사, 이직 등이나 프로젝트 완수, 학위 취득, 승진, 수상 등의 업적을 축하하기 위해서 작성한다. 축하 메시지를 통해 상대방에 대한 관심을 나타낼 수 있고 우호관계를 형성할 수 있다.

또한 사내외 소식지, 지역신문, 잡지 등을 항상 눈여겨봄으로써 축하 메시지를 작성할 기회를 찾아야 한다.

BUD ELECTRONICS COMPANY

3230 Polaris Avenue

Lexington, KY 40508

(606) 537-4937

February 2, 2008

Mrs. Dorothy Chang
Dorothy's Fabrics and Stuff
236 Victor Street
Lexington, KY 40508

Dear Dorothy,

Congratulations on being selected Businessman of the Year by the Lexington Chamber of Commerce.

If anyone is deserving of the honor, it is you with your tireless efforts to improve the downtown business area over the past several years. You did far more than anyone could expect of a businessman, and your efforts are really beginning to pay off.

Enclosed is a copy of the nice article about you that appeared in the Lexington News.

Dorothy, it is people like you who make Lexington such a nice place to live.

Sincerely,

Joe Vollmer

nc
Enclosure

## 예제 4

귀하의 동료인 Norma Fender는 full-time으로 일하면서 5년 동안 Charlotte Business College에서 야간수업을 수강해 왔고, 드디어 졸업과 함께 Advanced Office Service Certificate을 받게 되었다. 상황에 맞도록 아래 보기 중에서 적절한 단어를 골라서 밑줄을 채우시오.

stuck, accomplishment, set, reached, full-time, commended, completing, Advanced Office Services Certificate

Dear Norma,

Congratulations on _________ the requirements for an _________ _________ _________ _________ from Charlotte Business College!

It is not easy to work _________ and go to school at night. You are to be _________ for all your hard work and determination. You ______ a goal, and you _________ to it until you _________ it.

Norma, you should be proud of your _________. We need more people with ambition like yours.

Best wishes,

## D. Condolence Message(위로 메시지)

위로 메시지는 상대방이 가족이나 친지의 사망, 사고, 아픔 등 불행한 일을 당하여 큰 슬픔에 처하게 되었을 때 위로해주기 위하여 작성한다. 다른 이의 불행에 대하여 언급하는 것이 쉽지 않은 일이라 하더라도 위로의 메시지를 전달하여 상대방의 슬픔에 공감하고 감정적인 지원을 하고 있음을 알릴 필요가 있다. 단, 메시지가 어색하지 않도록 작성 시 유의한다.

### 위로 메시지의 예

Dear Mr. Summers,

I would like to extend the deep sympathy of all of us at Jason Associates.

We had the privilege of knowing and working with Edith for many years, and her friendly presence will be sadly missed.

Please consider us your friends and telephone us if we can be of any help.

Sincerely,

**기억하세요**

위로 메시지는 되도록 간결하면서도 진심어린 어조로 작성되어야 하며, 슬픔을 전달하는데 있어서 품위와 상대방에 대한 존경이 표현되어야 한다. "I'm sorry."라는 표현은 상투적이어서 진정성이 결여된 것처럼 들릴 수 있으므로 사용하지 않는다. 사망에 대한 위로 메시지의 경우 'death'라는 단어를 사용할 수는 있지만, 그것에 대한 자세한 설명은 불필요하다.

## 예제 5

Edith의 부재에 대한 위로 메시지이다. 상황과 문맥에 맞도록 알맞은 단어를 보기 중에서 골라 메시지를 완성하시오.

| lose, loss, sharing, shared, comfort, comfortable, before, ahead |
|---|

**Michael Barrett**

4368-83 Street, Brooklyn, New York 11214

Dear Hans,

Roseanne and I were deeply saddened to learn of your great ________. We hope the love you and Edith ________ will help ________ you in the days ________ .

If there is anything we can do for you now or in the future, please let us know.

With much sympathy,

Michael

UNIT 06

# Job-related Documents

(구직 관련 문서들)

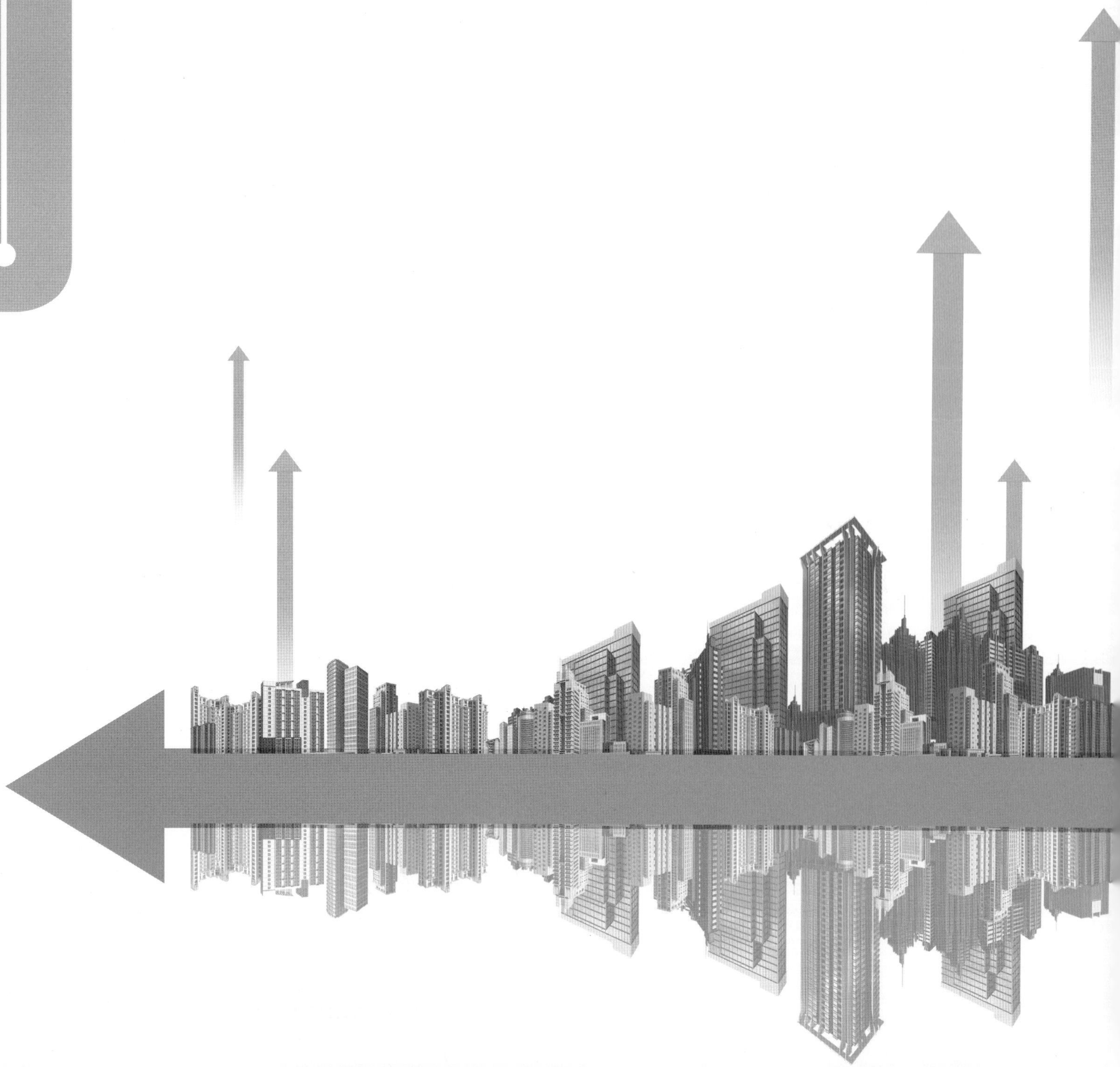

UNIT 06

# Job-related Documents
(구직 관련 문서들)

## 어휘 학습

| | |
|---|---|
| • resume | n. 이력서, 자기소개서 |
| • coverletter | n. 이력서 등을 송부할 때 첨부하는 표지 편지 |
| • detailed | a. 상세한, 세부에 걸친 |
| • schedule | v. 예정하다, 일정을 잡다 |
| • suitable | a. 적당한 |
| • entitled | a. ~라고 이름 지워진, 불리는 |
| • so-called | a. 소위, 이른바 |
| • marked | a. 두드러진, 주목받는 |
| • heckler | n. 삼빗 |
| • inner sanctum | 〈구어〉 서재 |
| • dictating machine | 구술 녹음기 |
| • assets | n. 재산, 자산 |
| • defendant | n. 피고 |
| • plaintiff | n. 원고, 고소인 |

## A. Resumes(영문 이력서)

### 1. Resumes란?

원하는 회사에 입사하기 위해서는 입사 원서와 영문 이력서를 작성하여 회사에 제출하고 interview에 임해야 한다.

영문 이력서는 일반적으로 Resumé라고 하지만 Personal History라고 쓰기도 한다. Resumé는 주소, 성명, 나이, 경력, 학력, 특기 등을 일목요연하게 추려서 쓴 것을 말하며, Personal History는 작문 형식으로 쓴 것을 말하는 것이 보통이다. Curriculum Vitae는 Personal History의 라틴어식 표현으로, 두 형식이 다 포함된 것이다.

### 2. Resumes의 구성요소

영문 이력서는 국문의 경우처럼 규격화된 일정한 양식은 없지만, 일반적으로 기준이 되고 있는 스타일과 반드시 기술해야 하는 내용은 다음과 같다.

#### 1) Personal Data(개인 정보)

이름, 주소, 전화번호, 생년월일, 성별 등으로 Identifying Information이라고 하기도 한다.

#### 2) Job Objective(희망 직종)

희망하는 직종과 직무로 Career Objective 또는 단순히 Objective라고도 하고, 미국에서는 Goal이라고도 한다. 입사 후 일하고 싶은 분야에 대한 자신의 적합성을 주로 기술한다.

#### 3) Qualifications(자격)

희망 직무에 대응하는 능력과 자질로 Capabilities라고도 한다.

#### 4) Education(학력)

Educational History, Educational Background라고 하기도 하며, 특별한 요구가 없는 한 최종 학력 두 가지 정도만 적으면 된다.

### 5) Work Experience(경력)

원칙적으로 최근의 사실부터 과거의 사실로 거슬러 올라가는 순서로 기록한다. 특히 경력자인 경우는 경력을 학력보다 먼저 적는다. 학생일 경우는 학력을 먼저 적는다. Employment History 또는 Work History 혹은 간단하게 Experience, Employment라고 할 때도 있다.

### 6) Activities(각종 활동 경력)

학교에서의 서클 활동(Extracurricular Activities)과 자원봉사 등 사회활동(Social Activities)을 요약해서 쓴다. 요즘에는 자원봉사 활동을 적극적으로 평가하는 기업이 많아지고 있다.

### 7) Skills, Hobbies(기술, 특기, 취미)

특히 희망하는 업무에 도움이 되는 기술이나 특기, 그리고 그 업무와 관련 있는 취미에 초점을 맞추어 쓴다.

### 8) Military Service(병역 관계)

방위 소집 복무자의 경우라면 제대 날짜를 표기하며 즉 병역 또는 방위 소집 면제자의 경우에는 'Exempted from Military Service'라고 쓴다.

### 9) Honors and Awards(상벌)

상벌 관계도 역시 교내 · 외적인 행사에서의 수상 경력이나 각종 표창 경력을 기록한다. Additional Remarks라고도 한다.

### 10) References(조회처)

이력서에는 우선 Available on request 또는 Furnished upon request(요구시 즉시 제출하겠음)라고 적어두면 된다. 이전 근무처의 상사나 대학의 지도 교수 등의 연락처, 신원 보증인이라기 보다는 본인의 능력이나 자질에 대해 보증할 수 있는 제3자를 말하며, 부모, 형제나, 친척은 해당되지 않는다.

## 3. Margin(이력서의 기본 여백)

일반적으로 여백의 폭은 사무실의 용지와 양식에 의한다.

문서의 기본 여백은 윗 부분을 2.5cm(1인치) 정도 여백을 두어 철(file)을 할 수 있게 하고, 아랫 부분은 적어도 1.5cm 정도 남겨 둔다. 좌우의 여백은 2~3cm 정도 남겨 두는데 오른쪽은 왼쪽보다 조금 좁게 남겨 두도록 한다.

이때 반드시 몇 cm라고 정해져 있는 것은 아니므로 편지의 내용이 적을 때는 여백을 널찍하게 잡아 본문의 모양이 중앙에 오도록 하는 것이 좋다. 보았을 때의 느낌이나 균형이 맞도록 보기 좋게 중앙에 오도록 조정하는 것이 좋다.

## Resume (1)

**YOUNG-HEE KIM**

103 MoonJung-dong, Songpa-ku, Seoul, 138-201, Korea (02) 525-7333

**OBJECTIVE**

Secretarial position with a Computer Company

**EDUCATION**

Han-kuk University, Seoul, Korea
Bachelor of Computer Science, February, 1996
Honors : GPA : 3.8
Presidential Scholarship (Four years)

**EXPERIENCE**

Part-time Job — September, 1995-February, 1996
Energy Research Institute, Seoul
* Programmer

Full-time Job — March, 1996-February, 1997
BIO Computer, Seoul
* Office Assistant

**ACTIVITIES**

Vice-President of Han-kuk
Secretary Club
Member of World Show
Drama Club

**RELATED COURSE WORK**

Word-processing
Computer Science
Programming
UNIX

References available upon request

## Resume (2)

# MIN-KYUNG CHOI

1410 Samsung-dong,
Kangnam-ku, Seoul
(02) 583-0825

**OBJECTIVE** A position as a Secretary

**EDUCATION** Graduated from Dong-bang High School, Seoul
Bu-chun College, Seoul Korea
--Secretarial Science Department, February, 1994

**ADDITIONAL COURSES :** Secretarial Office Procedure, Business English,
Word-processing, Information Processing,
Korean Shorthand, English Shorthand,

**EXPERIENCE**

| | |
|---|---|
| 6/92 - 8/96 | Office Assistant at Ted Co. |
| 5/95 - 5/96 | Receptionist at Hio Plaza |
| 3/94 - 3/95 | File Clerk and Office Assistant at Daemun Ltd. |

**SPECIAL SKILLS :** Speak fluent English
Word-processor, Spreadsheet, Database,
Shorthand (Korean, English)

**REFERENCES :** Jong-min Nam,
Chairman of ABC Company

## B. Coverletters(커버레터)

### 1. Coverletters란?

구직 편지의 목적은 구인측의 주의를 끌고 관심을 불러일으키고 면접 단계까지 발전시켜 약속을 얻어내기 위한 편지이다.
따라서 구직 편지에서는 첫째, 간결하게 특정 직종에 대한 구직 편지라는 사실을 명시한다. 둘째, 자신의 가장 큰 세일즈 포인트를 골라 그것이 구인측에 어떻게 도움이 되는지, 또 당신의 자격이 특정 업무에 어떻게 관련을 맺는지 피력한다. 셋째, 위에서 서술한 이외의 세일즈 포인트, 예를 들어 그 밖의 경력과 아르바이트 경험, 상대 회사나 관련 업무에 대한 관심 등에 대해서 언급한다.

### 2. Coverletter 작성 시 유의사항

구직 편지에 관한 체크 포인트는 아래와 같다. 귀하가 제출하는 구직 편지는 귀하가 비즈니스 문서를 쓰는 법을 어느 정도로 알고 있는가 하는 점을 나타내므로 이런 점을 충분히 체크하는 것이 중요하다.

#### 1) 외형

- 양질의 백지를 사용했는가?
- 올바른 형식인가?
- 매력적인 레이아웃인가?
- 오탈자, 문법적 오류나 지저분하게 된 곳은 없는가?

#### 2) 내용

- 취직하고자 하는 회사의 특정인 앞으로 쓰여진 것인가?
- 회신용 주소를 빠뜨리지 않았는가?
- 첫머리에서 읽는 사람의 주의를 끌고 있는가?
- 메시지를 가장 효과적으로 전달하는 언어를 담고 있는가?
- 구체적인 직종을 적었는가?

- 희망하는 이유를 적었는가?
- 자격이 있다고 믿는 이유를 적었는가?
- 최대 세일즈 포인트를 적었는가?
- 이력서 요점을 설명하고 있는가?
- 희망 직종과 관계가 있는 자격을 강조하고 있는가?
- 경험, 교육, 성격이 얼마나 도움이 되는지를 적었는가?
- 동봉한 이력서에 대해서 언급하고 있는가?
- 면접을 바라고 있는가?
- 전화번호와 받을 수 있는 시간을 적었는가?

### 3) 태도

- 구인 측의 입장을 고려하여 적었는가?
- 구직에 대해서 마음에서부터 우러나오는 관심이 있다는 사실을 나타내고 있는가?
- 제 1인칭의 사용은 가능한 피하고 있는가?
- 성실한 느낌을 주고 있는가?

## Coverletter (1)

115-3 Ssangmun-dong
Dobong-Ku, Seoul, 132-030

November 16, 2008

Mr. John Smith
Human Resources Director
TMB Inc.
949-1, Dogok-dong
Kangnam-Ku, Seoul, 135-270

Dear Mr. Smith :

I would like to apply for the position of secretary which was advertised in The Chosun Ilbo of November 15.

I have enclosed my resume, and I am very interested in working for your company. I will call you on November 25 to see if there are times available for an interview.

I look forward to talking with you.

Sincerely yours,

*Meehae Lee*
Mee-hae Lee

Enclosure

## Coverletter (2)

115-3 Ssangmun-dong

Dobong-Ku, Seoul, 132-030

November 16, 2008

Mr. John Smith

Human Resources Director

TMB Inc.

949-1, Dogok-dong

Kangnam-Ku, Seoul, 135-270

Dear Mr. Smith:

In the November 15th issue of The Chosun Ilbo, TMB Incorporated advertised that it was accepting applications for a secretarial position. I would like to apply for this position.

As you will see on the resume which I have enclosed, I have one year of secretarial experience and a detailed knowledge of the word processing programs, excel programs, and shorthand.

I am very interested in working for TMB Incorporated and would like to schedule an interview. I will call on November 25 to see if there are times available for an interview.

I am looking forward to meeting you.

Sincerely yours,

Mee-Hae Lee

Enclosure

## Reply to Application (1)

TMB Inc.
949-1 Dogok-dong
Kangnam-Ku, Seoul 135-270

November 20, 2008

Ms. Mee-hae Lee
115-3 Ssangmun-dong
Dobong-Ku, Seoul 132-030

Dear Ms. Lee :

We received your letter and resume on November 20.
We appreciate your interest in the TMB Inc.
We would like to schedule an interview at 9 a.m on Tuesday, November 25. Please call and let us know if this is also suitable for you.

Again, thank you for your interest in TMB, Inc.
We look forward to talking with you.

Sincerely yours,

John Smith
Human Resources Director

# Reply to Application (2)

TMB Inc.
949-1 Dogok-dong
Kangnam-Ku, Seoul 135-270

November 20, 2008

Ms. Mee-hae Lee
115-3 Ssangmun-dong
Dobong-ku, Seoul 132-030

Dear Ms. Lee :

We received your letter and resume on November 20. We appreciate your interest in TMB Incorporated.

We are interested in learning more about your secretarial experience and would like to schedule an interview. We have time available at 9 a.m. on Tuesday, November 25. Please call and let us know if this time also suitable for you.

Again, thank you for your interest in TMB, Inc. We look forward to meeting you.

Sincerely yours,

John Smith
Human Resources Director

## 문법 따라잡기 : 따옴표 (") 와 이탤릭체

### 1. 따옴표

**1)** 따옴표는 원칙적으로 다른 사람이 쓴 글이나 말한 것을 그대로 옮겨 올 때 사용한다. 짧은 직접 인용문이 문장 앞이나 뒤에 위치할 때에는 콤마를 사용한다.

- The executive announced, "An important project start in January."
- "A special campaign will begin in March," the president announced.

직접 인용문이 길거나, 독립된 절 다음에 놓일 때에는 콤마 대신에 콜론을 인용문 앞에 찍는다.

- Ms. Jones stated : "If Mr. Tucker completes the first draft of the contract by noon, I will be able to type it by five. If he doesn't, I'll have to type it tomorrow."
- She said this : "You have to follow my suggestion."

직접 인용문 사이에 다른 문장이나 구가 삽입되면, 인용문은 모두 따옴표로 묶고, 삽입구 앞뒤에 쉼표를 찍어 구별한다.

- "Not a bad profit," my partner said, "for a company that was organized only a year ago."

**2)** 간접 인용문에는 따옴표를 사용하지 않는다.
간접 인용문은 주로 that 이나 if, whether 등과 함께 쓰인다.

- The president announced that a special campaign will begin in March. (간접화법)
- The president announced, "A special campaign will begin in March." (직접법)
- Mr. Kim asked me if I be willing to work overtime. (간접화법)
- Mr. Ross asked, "Do you want to work more?" (직접화법)

**3)** 문장 내에서 특정 표현이나 용어의 의미를 강조하기 위해서 따옴표를 사용하기도 한다.

① 뒤에 나오는 표현을 강조하는 entitled, so-called, marked, 또는 signed 와 같은 단어 다음에 따옴표를 쓴다.

- Please explain the managing of the people entitled "N-Generation".
- The parcel was market "Fragile".

② 문장 안에서의 의미가 아니라 단어나 어구 자체를 의미할 때에는 그 단어를 따옴표로 묶거나 밑줄을 친다.

- Many people overuse the phrase "you know".
- Both and and or could be used in that sentence.

③ 전문, 학술용어 등의 친숙하지 않은 언어가 처음 나올 때 그 용어에 따옴표를 사용한다.

- Many secretaries enclose "Courtesy carbon" for a reader's convenience.

④ 글을 흥미롭게 하기 위해 고의적인 문법적 오류, 속어, 유머, 등을 사용할 때에도 따옴표를 찍는다.

- The speaker told a heckler to "cool it."
- He took the visitors into his "inner sanctum."
- It "don't matter" at all.

⑤ 외국어를 번역할 때에는 외국어에는 밑줄을 치고(인쇄물에서는 이탤릭체로), 번역된 의미에는 따옴표를 찍는다.

- "Have a good trip!" is often replaced by the french expression "Bonvoyage."
- Aloha means "hello."

### 4) 인용문 안의 인용문

인용문 안에서 다시 인용할 때는 작은따옴표를 사용한다.

- The advisor mentioned, "We must execute the project business process reengineering as soon as possible."
- "Try to collect," Mr. Brown said, "all accounts I have marked 'past due'."

### 5) 제목이나 타이틀

강의, 기사, 에세이, 그림, (책의 챕터 제목) 등에 따옴표를 사용한다.

- I read the article entitled "How to Develop Human Resource" in Harvard Business Review.
- The lecturer's topic was "It's Never Late"

책, 잡지, 신문 등의 인쇄물과 연극, 영화, 오페라 등의 공연물의 제목은 따옴표로 묶지 않고, 이탤릭체로 쓰거나, 밑줄을 긋거나, 전체를 대문자로 쓴다.

- We ran an ad in The New York Times. Or THE NEW YORK TIMES or The New York Times.
- Pretty Woman was a successful Hollywood romantic comedy movie. Or PRETTY WOMAN or Pretty Woman.

### 6) 따옴표 안의 표현에서의 구두법

❶ 마침표와 콤마는 항상 닫는 따옴표 안쪽에 찍는다.

- Some dictating machines record by "computer media recorder."
- "Our dictating machine records in computer file." one secretary said.

❷ 콜론과 새미콜론은 항상 닫는 따옴표 바깥에 위치한다.

- The following are listed under "Assets": cash, equipment, and accounts receivable.
- The person who is being sued is known as the "defendant"; one who is bringing the suit, as the "plaintiff."

❸ 물음표와 느낌표는 때로는 닫는 따옴표 안쪽에, 때로는 바깥에 위치한다.

- Patric shouted "Stop!" when he saw Johnson.
- He asked, "Do you know what time it is?"

- Where did you put the file labeled "miscellaneous".
- How careless of you to drop a package marked "Fragile"!

## 2. 이탤릭체

❶ 책, 잡지, 신문, 팜플렛, 시의 제목은 이탤릭체로 표시한다.

- The *Wallstreet Journal* gave an impressive review to Bill Gate's latest book.

❷ 영화, TV 프로그램, 연극 등의 예술 작품의 이름을 이탤릭체로 쓴다.

- Ms. Lee has seen *Cats* over ten times.
- I think *Doctor Jibago* is the greatest movie.

③ 배, 기차, 비행기, 우주선의 이름을 이탤릭체로 쓴다.

- The *Lady Victoria* sailed from New York on Tuesday.
- *Apollo Nine* was placed in orbit exactly as scheduled.

④ (영어가 아닌) 외국 단어나 어구를 이탤릭체로 쓴다.

- Everybody called her performance *tŕes* bien.

⑤ 문장 안에서 의미를 갖지 않고, 단어, 글자, 숫자 그 자체로 쓰일 때에는 이탤릭체를 사용한다.

- When writing contracts, you should cross all your *t's*.
- You must not confuse the word *personne*l with the *personal*.
- Don't misregard '*G*' as '*6*' reading this document.

## 연습문제 – 따옴표와 이탤릭체

올바른 위치에 따옴표를 찍거나 이탤릭체로 고쳐 쓰시오. 문장을 고칠 필요가 없으면 C 라고 표시하시오.

1. Sunflower is title of one of Van Gogh's most famous paintings.

2. Mandy told Edward that she was planning to spend holiday in Florida next year.

3. The Japanese dinner we had last night was "Subarashi".

4. When I said good morning to Samuel he replied Guten Tag.

5. Please speak to me more slowly, pleaded Sarah.

6. Watch out, he said excitedly, you're about to sit on a wet chair!

7. The newspaper article that the editor..."How to invest safety."

8. Man of Lamancha was one of the best musical productions that I have over seen.

9. Maggie asked me if I wanted to enroll the cheerleading club committee.

10. Snow White is the name of our sailboat.

11. The flight attendant told us to fasten our seat belts immediately.

12. What happened to all the ice cream? asked Tim.

## C. 기타 구인구직 관련 편지들

### 1. 인터뷰 기회를 준 것에 대한 감사편지

- 최대한 신속하게 답신한다.
- 인터뷰 일정이 변경될 수 있으므로, 개인 연락처를 두 개 이상 명시해 둔다.

Dear Ms. Kennedy:

Thanks for your prompt response to my letter. As we had previously discussed, I will meet you in your offices on Thursday, March 22, at 2 p.m. If you have to change the appointment, you can phone me on my private line at 123-456-7890 or send an e-mail to my personal account.
The address is: kyc3@daelim.ac.kr

I look forward to meeting you and continuing our discussion in person!

Sincerely,

## 2. Job Offer를 수락하는 편지

- 급여, 복리후생, 근무시간, 보험제도 등을 포함한 고용조건을 언급해야 함
- 필요한 경우 고용계약서를 요청할 것
- 업무와 회사에 대한 열정을 보여줄 것

Dear Mr. Johns:

Thanks for your call today.
I accept your offer of a position as advertising manager at a salary of $38,000 a year. Based on our phone conversation, I understand that in addition to Oak Engineering's standard benefits plan, I will receive two weeks of vacation the first year. As discussed, I will also be given a private office (not a cubicle) with a PC, fax, and printer. I will share an administrative assistant with Joe Bulges, your trade show manager. My starting date will be Monday, August 21. Oak will reimburse me for mover's fees for relocating from Baltimore to Secaucus.

If I have understood the terms of my employment correctly, please sign in the space provided below and return to me in the enclosed self-addressed stamped envelope.

I'm thrilled about starting with Oak and look forward to a long and productive relationship. On a personal note, I'm also delighted that you're going to be my boss!

Sincerely,

Agreed : ______________________ Date : ______________________

## 3. Job Offer를 불가피하게 거절하는 편지

- 제안을 수락할 수 없음을 최대한 빨리 알린다.
- 거절할 수밖에 없는 이유를 간략하게 알리되 다른 회사와 비교하는 표현을 피할 것

Dear Kathy,

Thanks for your call. However, after much thought, I have decided to take a position with General Publishing in Flint, and must turn down your generous offer.

I'm sure I would have enjoyed working with you and the Innovative Design Group. But the opportunity with General Publishing was as a Management position, which you know I had aspirations to. This position is more in line with my career objectives than the staff position you had available.

I'm sure we will meet again, perhaps at the upcoming Innovative Design Society Conference. Perhaps we can meet at your booth for a cup of coffee-on me, of course.

Sincerely,

## 4. 사직할 때

- 사직하게 됨을 알리고 정확한 사직일자를 명시(사직의 이유를 알릴 것인지는 선택사항임)
- 후임을 찾을 때까지 근무할 것임을 알리되 최종 기한을 반드시 명시해야 함
- 회사에서의 근무 경험이 매우 가치 있었다고 언급함으로써 우호관계 유지

Dear Mr. Nakamura:

This letter is to notify you that I'm resigning from my position at Global Affiliates to take a new position at Associated Systems.

My last day will be October 31. By giving you six weeks notice I'm hoping to provide you with some extra time to find a replacement. After October 31, I'll still be available if you need help locating resources or getting answers to any questions the new employee may have about procedures or records. You will be able to reach me at my new number, 123-456-7890.

For the record, I enjoyed my job and our association here at Global.
But the position at Associated has significantly higher compensation, and in our annual reviews, you indicated the salary for someone in my classification could not come near this level. So the decision is mainly a financial one. However, I'll miss you and the whole group in our department.

Sincerely,

## 5. 현재 공석이 없음을 알릴 때

- 회사에 관심을 가져 준 데에 대한 감사 표현
- 현재 공석이 없음을 직접적으로 언급(모호하거나 오해를 일으킬 수 있는 표현을 피할 것)
- 지원자의 이력서를 보관해 두고 추후에 공석이 나면 참조하겠다고 약속할 것

Dear Mr. Baker:

Your letter of inquiry about employment opportunities in our company was forwarded to me from human resources because of your interest in obtaining a position in quality assurance. I am pleased you thought of Remco Widgets.

At this time, all our supervisory slots in manufacturing and production are filled, and the job responsibilities in those positions include quality assurance. I do not think there will be an opening for a manager dedicated to quality assurance this year.

I will ask Human Resources to keep your letter on file, since you certainly seem qualified in the QA field. If you don't hear from them, call Ronny Bruce, our Personnel Manager, in April to see if anything has opened up for you.

Sincerely,

## 6. 불합격 통보

- 지원자의 경력이나 자질에 대한 칭찬
- 간단하지만 명확하게 불합격 통보(불합격 이유를 자세하게 나열할 필요는 없다.)
- 지원해 준 것에 대한 감사 표현

Dear Mr. Lim:

It was a pleasure to meet with you last weeks in our offices at Integrated Network Solutions, Inc. Your programming background and corporate experience give you skills that will be useful in many IS positions.

We have reviewed your credentials but unfortunately do not find a suitable match between your background and experience and the opening in our company.

Thank you for your interest in our company. Good luck in your job search.

Sincerely,

## 예제 1

다음 영문 커버레터를 읽고 아래의 보기에서 적절한 단어를 찾아서 밑줄을 채우시오.

consideration, enclosed, includes, past, possibility, coverletter, recent, resume, including, possible

Dear Ms. Collins:

As my ______ resume, I am a ______ graduate of Daelim College with a major in Secretarial Administration. My experience ______ an internship with a large publishing company and word processing a novel for a best-selling author. I would like to meet with you to discuss the ______ of gaining an entry-level secretarial position with your company. I will call you on Tuesday, October 2 to discuss the possibility of an interview.

My ______ is enclosed. Thanks for your time and ______.

Sincerely,

## 예제 2

다음 영문이력서 내용에 맞게 밑줄을 채우시오.

**Jane Kim**

123-1, Bisan 1-dong, Dongan-gu,
Anyang-si, Gyeonggi-do, Korea
Mobile: (011) 467-4700
E-mail: webmster@daelim.ac.kr

__________ : Medical Secretary/ Hospital Reservation Coordinator

__________ :

- More than 2 years experience as a medical secretary for both large and mid-sized hospitals
- Expertise in promoting open communication with staff members.
- English: Speaking, reading, and writing competence.

__________ :

2006-present
Medical Assistant, Sam-Hwan Hospital

__________ :

B.S. (1999)
Secretarial Administration, Hankang University

__________ :

Available upon request

## 예제 3

다음의 구직광고를 참고하여, Administrative Assistant 포지션에 지원하는 커버레터를 작성하시오.

| JOB OPPORTUNITY |
| --- |
| **Administrative Assistant**<br><br>A leading multinational company is looking for an Administrative Assistant position.<br>Ideal candidate must have at least 2 or 3 years of experience as well as excellent command of English. Interested candidated are required to send resumes via e-mail by October 28, Friday, 5:00 p.m. to:<br><br>Attn : Human Resources Manager<br>e-mail : hr@mnm.com |

UNIT 07

# Company Organization

(기업 조직 관련 용어와 문서들)

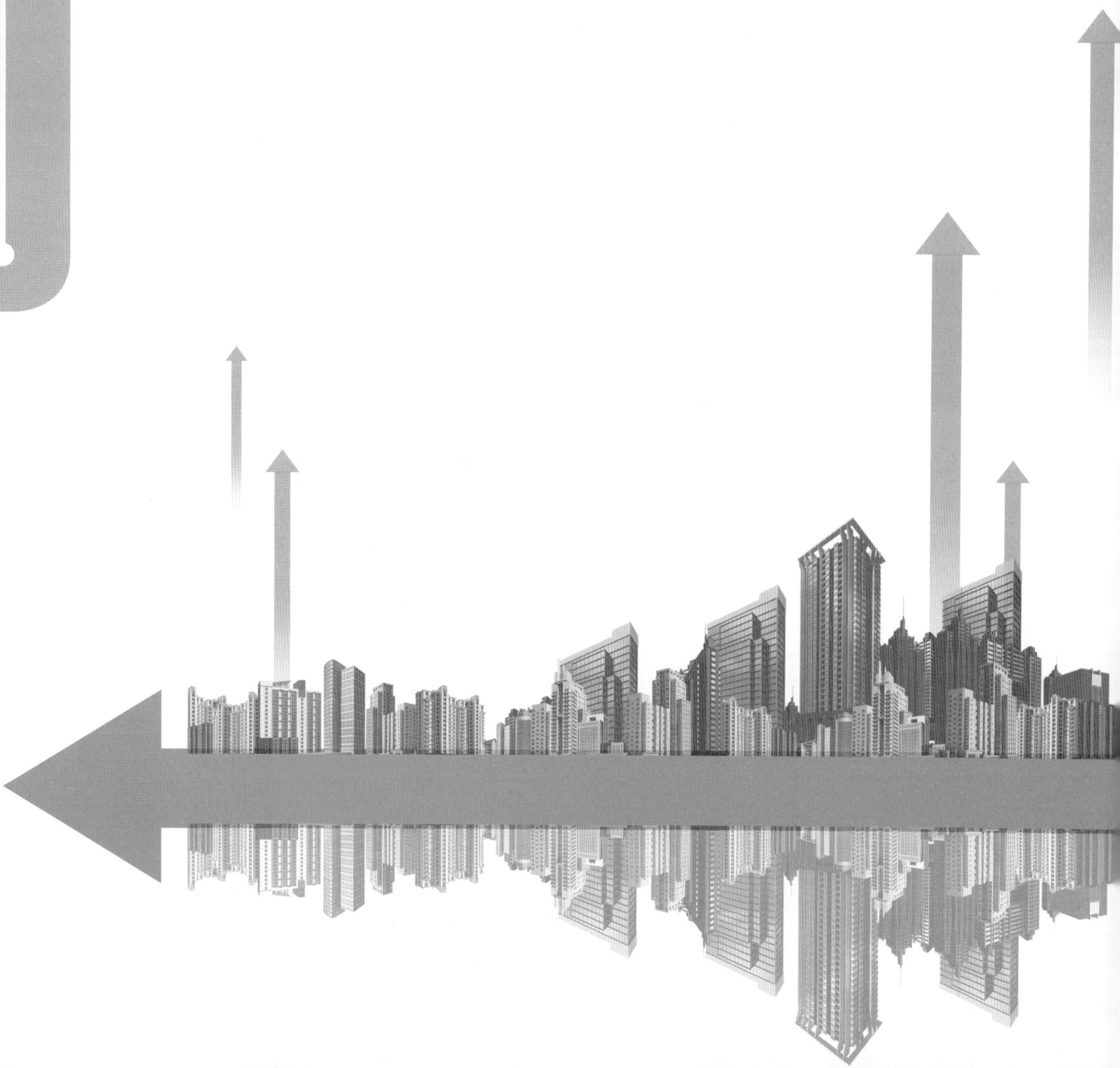

UNIT 07

# Company Organization

(기업 조직 관련 용어와 문서들)

## 어휘 학습

- organizational — showing the way a company is organised
  a. (회사, 기관 등의)조직의, 구조의 n. organization
- structure — n. 조직구조
- Managing Director — director who is in charge of a whole company
  n. 총괄이사, 대표이사, 혹은 상무
- executives — people who put decisions into action
  n. 회사의 중역, 간부
- personnel — staff
  n. 인사
- training — teaching employees how to do something
  n. 훈련
- rationalization — making more efficient
  n. 합리화, 효율화
- region — part of a country/an area
  n. 조직, 구역
- split — divide
  v. 나누다

| | |
|---|---|
| • matrix (basis) | organised according to two sets of criteria, e.g. geographical and functional<br>n. 매트릭스 조직 |
| • section | part of a company<br>n. 구역, 부문 |
| • subsidiary | company which is owned by a parent company<br>n. 자회사 |
| • affiliate | company wholly or partly owned by another company<br>n. 관계사 |
| • corporate | referring to a whole company<br>n. 회사, 기업 |
| • appointment | arrangement to meet<br>n. 약속 |
| • approach | contact someone<br>v. 다가가다, 접근하다 |
| • investment | placing of money so that it will increase in value<br>n. 투자 |
| • convenient | suitable<br>a. 편리한 |
| • suit | be suitable or convenient<br>v. 적합하다 |
| • current | present<br>a. 현재의 |
| • prospectus | document which gives information to buyers or customers<br>n. 사업설명서 |
| • up-to-date | informed of the latest information<br>a. 최신의 |
| • project | plan<br>n. 사업계획, 프로젝트 |
| • user | person who uses something<br>n. 사용자 |

| | |
|---|---|
| • accounting | concerned with the work of recording money paid and received<br>n. 회계 |
| • install | put (a machine) into an office or a factory<br>v. 설치하다 |
| • automated | worked automatically by machine<br>a. 자동화된 |
| • assembly line | production system where the product moves slowly through the factory with new sections added to it as it goes along<br>n. 조립라인 |
| • recruitment | looking for new staff<br>n. 신입사원 모집 |
| • to rationalise | to make more efficient<br>v. 효율화하다 |
| • distribution | way of sending goods<br>n. 유통 |
| • network | system which links different places, e.g. warehouses, together<br>n. 네트워크 |
| • cut | sudden lowering of costs<br>n. (비용)삭감 |
| • series | group<br>n. 시리즈, 그룹 |
| • target | level, e.g. of sales, to aim for<br>n. 목표치 |
| • performance | how good or bad the results are<br>n. 성과 |
| • product | thing which is made or manufactured<br>n. 제품 |
| • launch | put a new product on the market<br>v. 출시하다 |
| • peak | highest point<br>n. 최고의 |

| | |
|---|---|
| • unit | single product<br>n. 단품 |
| • steadily | in a regular or continuous way<br>ad. 꾸준히 |
| • settle | stay at the same level<br>v. 유지하다 |
| • rapidly | quickly<br>ad. 신속하게 |
| • slightly | not very much, a little<br>ad. 조금씩 |
| • results | outcome of the year's trading<br>n. 결과 |
| • roughly | about, approximately<br>ad. 대략 |
| • promotion | advertising, publicity<br>n. 홍보, 판촉 |
| • push | promote vigorously<br>v. 적극적으로 판촉하다 |
| • optimistic | feeling sure that things will work out well<br>a. 낙관적인 |
| • achieve | succeed in doing something<br>v. 성취하다 |
| • medium-term | referring to a period of about five years<br>a. 중장기적인 |
| • chairman | person who is in charge of a meeting<br>n. 회장 |
| • review | general examination<br>n. 검토 |
| • turnover | amount of sales<br>n. 판매량, 총 매출액 |

- drop — fall
  v. 떨어지다, 급락하다
- profits — money gained which is more than money spent
  n. 이윤
- domestic — home
  a. 지역의, 가정의, 국내의
- competitive — difficult, as a result of the activities of other companies in the same area
  a. 경쟁적인
- disappointing — below expectation
  a. 실망을 주는
- policy — decisions on the way of doing something
  n. 정책
- actually — in fact
  ad. 사실은
- recruit — get new staff
  v. 신규채용하다
- expand — get bigger
  v. 확장하다
- quality assurance — checking that the quality of a product is good
  n. 품질관리
- growth — increase in size
  n. 성장
- prototype — first model of a new machine before it goes into production
  n. 시제품
- strategy — plan of future action
  n. 전략
- define — find
  v. 정의하다
- flexible — can be changed
  a. 융통성 있는

- objective — something which you aim for
  n. 목적
- market share — percentage of a total market which the sales of a company or product cover
  n. 시장점유율
- reduce — make less or smaller
  v. 감소하다, 줄이다
- margins — difference between the buying and selling price
  n. 이윤
- long-term — for a long period of time
  a. 장기적인
- prospect — possibility for the future
  n. 가망
- plant — factory
  n. 공장
- manufacturing — production
  n. 생산
- upgrade — make better, to improve
  v. 개선하다
- to adapt — to change
  v. 적응시키다, 맞추다
- sub-contract — agree with another company that they will do part of the work
  v. 하도급 계약을 하다
- competition — trying to do better than another company
  n. 경쟁
- competitor — person or company who tries to do better than another person or company
  n. 경쟁자
- enter the market — start to do business
  v. 시장에 진입하다

| | |
|---|---|
| • to grow | to become bigger<br>v. 증가 |
| • weakness | position of not being strong or active<br>n. 약점 |
| • major | important, big<br>a. 주요한 |
| • return | official report of income and profits<br>n. 수익 |
| • to overtake | to pass<br>v. 따라잡다, 추월하다 |
| • reliable | can be trusted<br>a. 믿을 수 있는 |
| • reputation | general opinion about something or someone<br>n. 명성 |
| • to hold on to | to keep<br>v. 유지하다 |
| • construction | building<br>n. 건설 |
| • pilot study | test which, if successful, will be expanded into a full operation<br>n. 파일럿 스터디 예행 |
| • last | take time<br>v. 지속하다, 시간이 걸리다 |
| • contractor | person or company working according to a written agreement<br>n. 계약자 |
| • schedule | plan the time when something will happen<br>v. 일정을 잡다 |
| • sign | write one's name on a document to approve or accept it<br>n. 서명하다 |
| • contract | legal agreement between two parties<br>n. 계약 |
| • stage | step n. 단체 |

- foundations
  base of a building put deep into the ground to support the walls
  n. 설립
- tight (schedule)
  leaving no extra time at all to put right mistakes or fix difficulties
  a. 빡빡한
- pharmaceutical
  relating to drugs used in medical treatment
  a. 약학의, 약국의, 약제의
- unanimously
  of one mind; without dissent
  ad. 만장일치로
- commendation
  an official award usually given as formal public statement
  n. 추천, 상, 칭찬
- revenue
  the entire amount of income
  n. 총 소득액, 총수입
- subsequent
  following in time or order
  n. 다음의, 뒤이어 일어나는

## 1. 조직과 관련된 표현

이번 장에서는 회사 및 기타 조직과 관련된 어휘를 다음의 다섯 가지 측면에서 학습해 볼 것이다.

- hierarchy(계층, 보고체계)
- responsibilities/functions(업무, 직무)
- titles(직함)
- affiliates(관계사)
- structure(조직구조)

각 조직의 직책이나 부서명은 기관에 따라 다소 차이가 있으나 대체적인 표현방식은 아래와 같다.

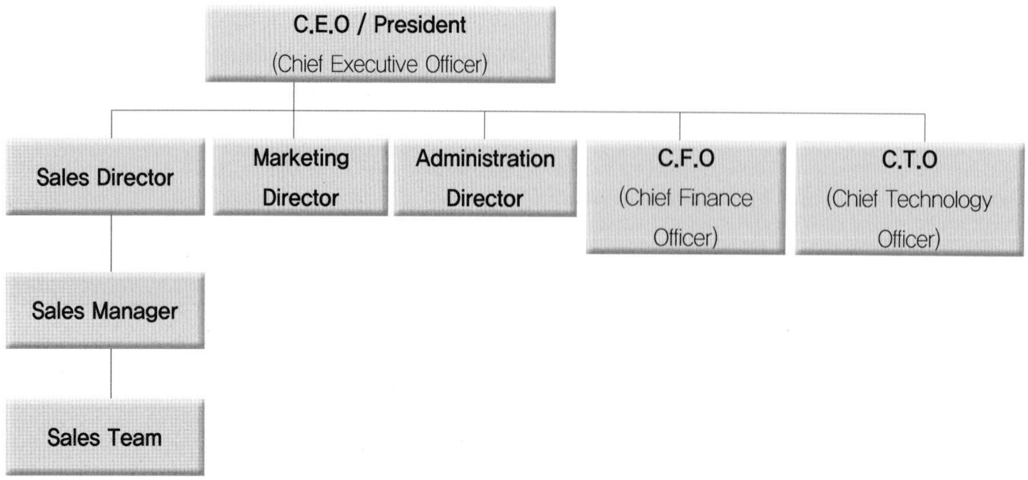


The company **is headed by** C.E.O — 회사는 대표이사가 **이끌어 간다**.

The Sales Director **reports to** C.E.O — 영업이사는 대표이사에게 **보고한다**.

The Marketing Director **is under** the President. — 영업이사는 대표이사 **직속이다**.

C.T.O **is accountable to** C.E.O — 영업이사는 대표이사에게 **보고 의무가 있다**.

The Sales Director **is supported by** a sales team. — 영업이사는 영업부원의 **지원을 받는다**.

The Sales Director **is assisted by** an Assistant Sales Manager. — 영업이사는 영업과장의 **보조를 받는다**.

## 1. Responsibilities/functions(업무, 직무)

| | |
|---|---|
| The Finance Department **is responsible for** accounting. | 재무부서는 회계를 **책임지고 있다**. |
| The R&D (Research and Development) Department **takes care of** new product development. | R&D 부서는 신제품 개발을 **맡고 있다**. |
| The Administration Manager **is in charge of** personnel. | 총무과장은 인사를 **책임지고 있다**. |

## 2. Titles(직함) 및 Departments(부서명)

| | | | |
|---|---|---|---|
| Chairman | 회장 | President | 사장 |
| Executive Managing Director | 전무 | Vice President | 부사장 |
| Senior Vice-President | 수석부사장 | Chief Executive Officer | 최고경영자(CEO) |
| Managing Director | 상무 | Finance Director | 재무이사 |
| Sales Director | 영업이사 | Sales Manager | 영업부장(과장) |

| | |
|---|---|
| General Affairs Department Administrative Division | 총무부 |
| Finance Department | 재무부 |
| Accounting Department | 경리부, 회계부 |
| Sales Department | 영업부 |
| Personnel Department | 인사부 |
| Purchasing Department | 구매부 |
| Marketing Department | 마케팅부 |
| Production Department | 제조부(생산부) |
| Public Relations Department | 홍보부 |
| Public Advertising Department | 광고부 |
| Planning & Coordination Department | 기획조정실 |
| Research & Development Department | 연구개발부 |
| Overseas Enterprise Department | 해외사업부 |
| Elcctronic Data Processing Department | 전산실 |
| Head office, Main Office, Headquarter | 본사 |
| Branch Office | 지점 |

**기억하세요**

회장(Chairman)과 이사(Directors)는 회사의 "이사회"(Board of Directors, Executive Board)를 구성한다.

### 3. Affiliates(관계사)

X is the **parent company**.

X는 **모회사**이다.

A, B, and C are **subsidiaries**(more than 50% owned by the parent).

(A, B, C는 **자회사**이다. -- 모회사가 50% 이상의 지분을 소유하고 있을 때)

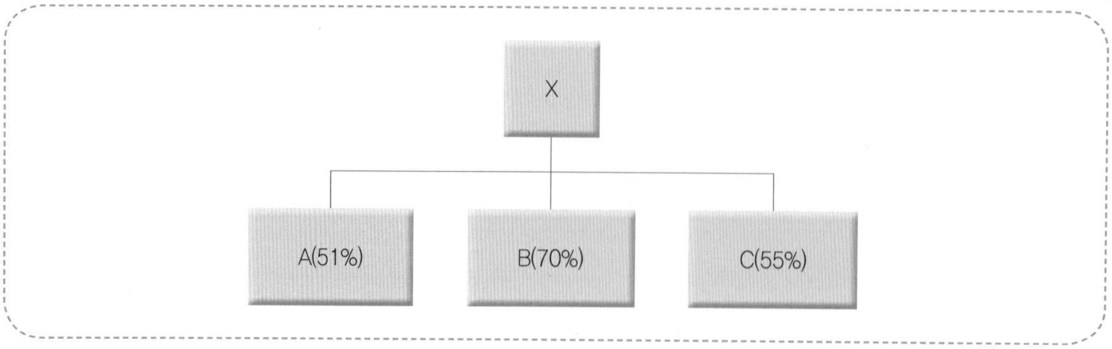


### 4. Structure(조직구조)

The Car Division **consists of** the Production Department and the Sales Department.

자동차 사업부는 생산부와 영업부로 **구성된다**.

The Production Department **comprises** the Methods Section and the Maintenance Section.

생산부는 절차 파트와 유지보수 파트로 **이루어진다**.

The Sales Department is **made up of** the Advertising Section and the After-sales Section.

영업부는 광고 파트와 애프터세일즈 파트로 **구성된다**.

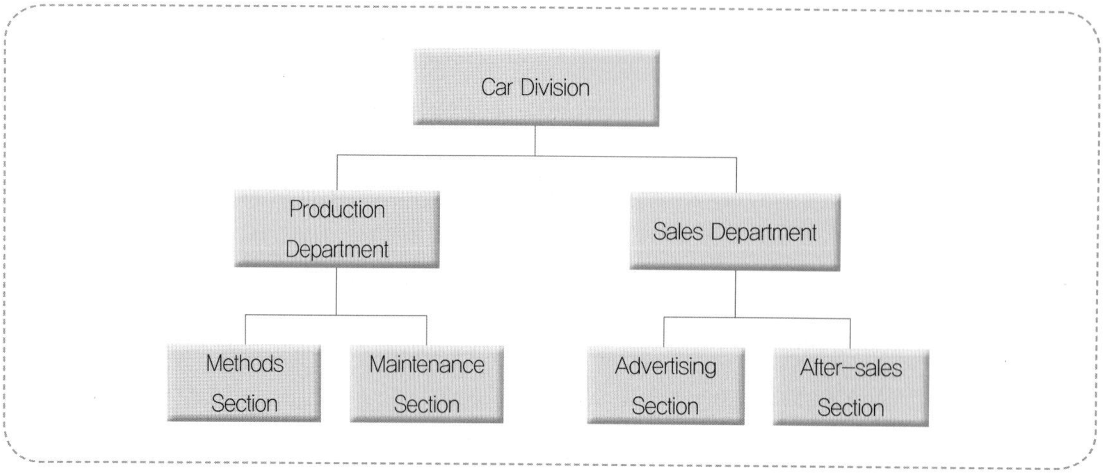

## 5. Business Activities(비즈니스 표현들)

비즈니스 상황에서 주로 쓰이는 표현을 학습한다.

### 1) 그래프 묘사하기

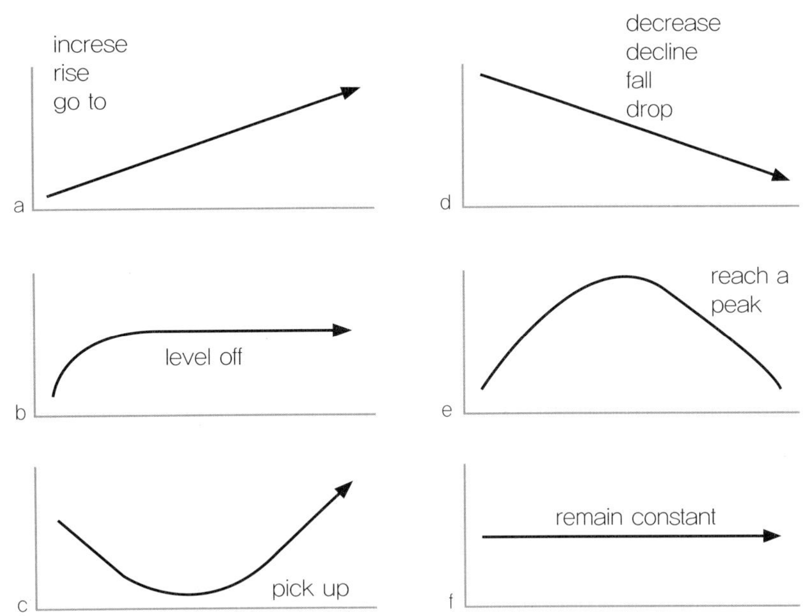


1. Sales **reached** a peak just one year after launch.
   출시 단 1년 후에 매출은 최고치를 달성했다

2. The following two years sales **slightly dropped**.
   다음 2년 동안은 매출이 약간 감소했다

3. Then sales **fell** to 500,000 won by the end of year five
   매출은 5차년도 말까지 500,000원으로 떨어졌다

4. Last year sales **increased** to 800,000 won
   작년에는 매출이 800,000원까지 증가했다

## 2) 실적 보고

1. Turnover **increased** by 14% last year.
   총매출액은 작년에 14% 까지 증가했다

2. The company **had** disappointing results recently.
   회사는 최근 실망스러운 실적을 보였다

3. The domestic consumer market **has been** very competitive.
   내수소비시장은 매우 (지금까지) 경쟁적이었다.

4. Two years ago we **launched** an updated product.
   2년 전에 우리(회사)는 개선된 제품을 출시했다.

5. We **recruited** 20 managers.
   우리(회사)는 스무 명의 관리자를 신규 채용했다.

## 3) 기업전략

1. If we **reduce** prices, our market Share will **increase**.
   우리 회사 제품의 가격을 내리면, 시장점유율이 증가할 것이다.

2. If we can **reduce** unit costs, That must **put** us **in a strong position**.
   우리 제품의 단가를 낮추면, 우리가 유리한 위치를 점하게 될 것이다.

3. Unit costs can **come down** if we **invest** in new plant.
   새 공장에 투자하면, 단가가 내려갈 수 있다.

## 2. 기관별 조직도

기관별 영어 조직도를 살펴보고 각 조직 구조의 특성과 영문 직책명을 학습한다.

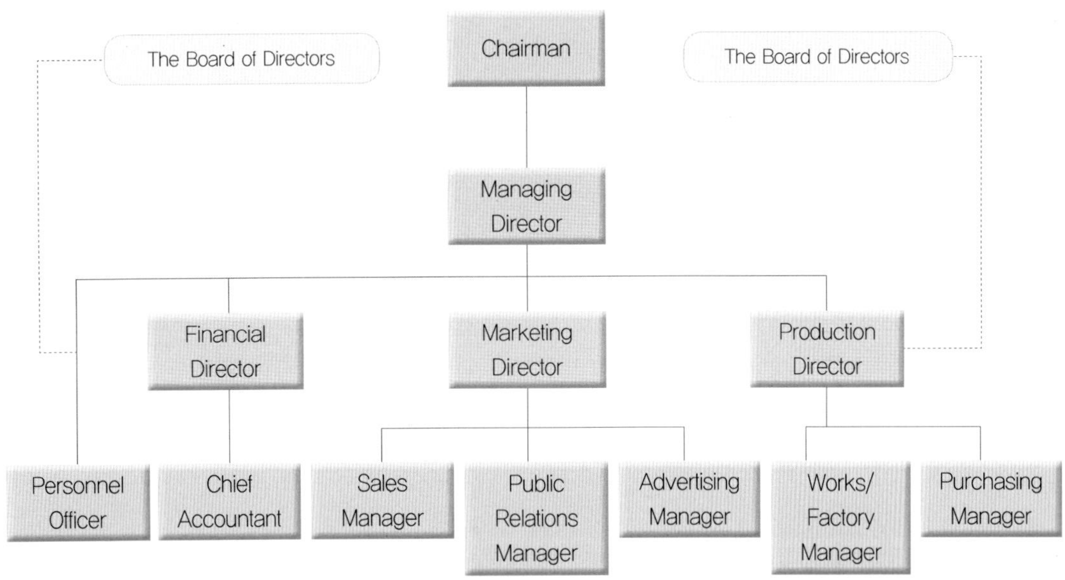


### 1. 물류회사 조직도의 예

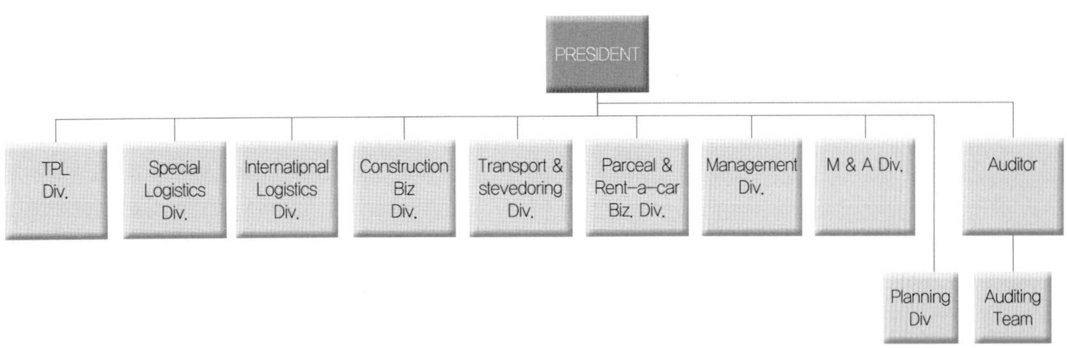

## 2. 제약회사 조직도의 예

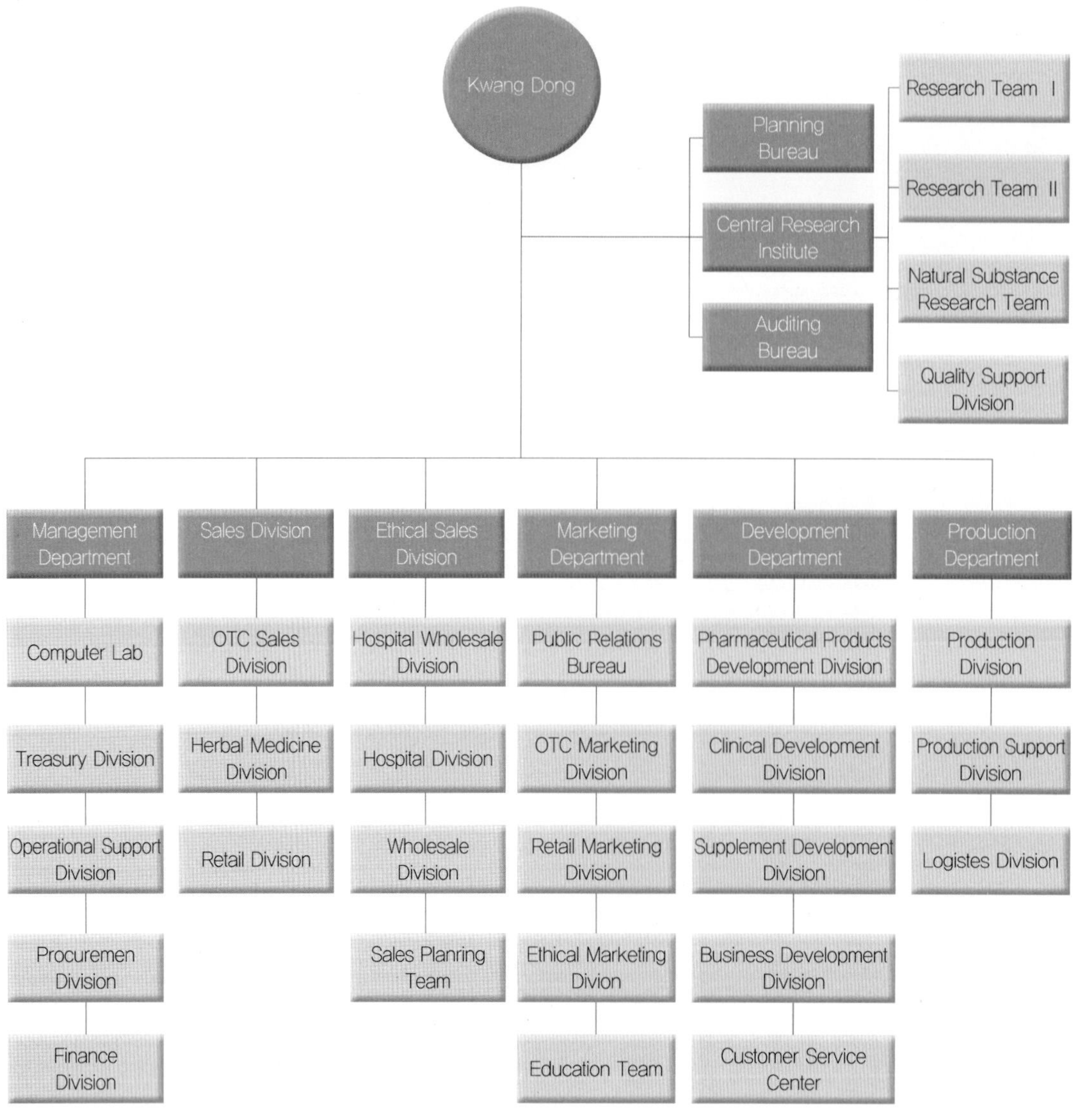
Kwang Dong
Planning Bureau
Central Research Institute
Auditing Bureau
Research Team Ⅰ
Research Team Ⅱ
Natural Substance Research Team
Quality Support Division
Management Department
Sales Division
Ethical Sales Division
Marketing Department
Development Department
Production Department
Computer Lab
Treasury Division
Operational Support Division
Procuremen Division
Finance Division
OTC Sales Division
Herbal Medicine Division
Retail Division
Hospital Wholesale Division
Hospital Division
Wholesale Division
Sales Planring Team
Public Relations Bureau
OTC Marketing Division
Retail Marketing Division
Ethical Marketing Divion
Education Team
Pharmaceutical Products Development Division
Clinical Development Division
Supplement Development Division
Business Development Division
Customer Service Center
Production Division
Production Support Division
Logistes Division

## 3. 병원 조직도의 예 1

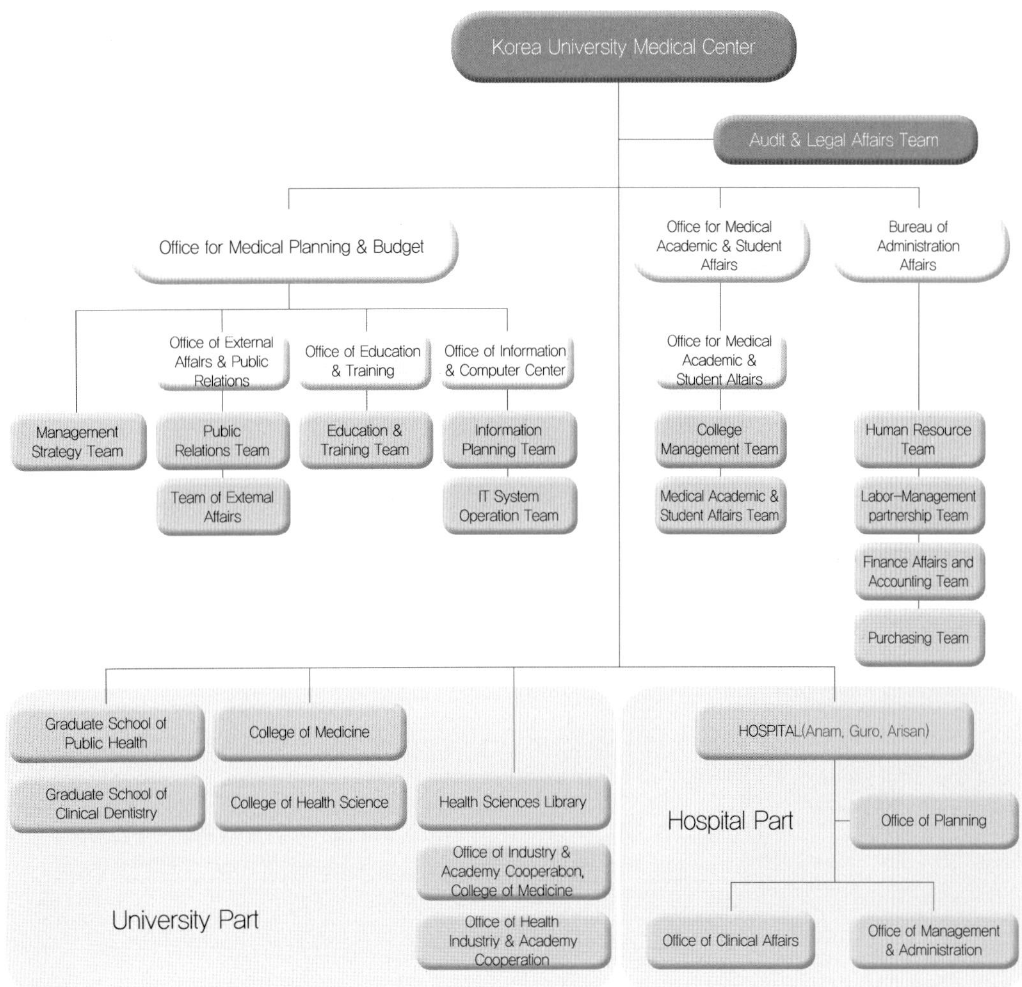
Korea University Medical Center
Audit & Legal Affairs Team
Office for Medical Planning & Budget
Office for Medical Academic & Student Affairs
Bureau of Administration Affairs
Management Strategy Team
Office of External Affairs & Public Relations
Office of Education & Training
Office of Information & Computer Center
Public Relations Team
Team of External Affairs
Education & Training Team
Information Planning Team
IT System Operation Team
Office for Medical Academic & Student Affairs
College Management Team
Medical Academic & Student Affairs Team
Human Resource Team
Labor-Management partnership Team
Finance Affairs and Accounting Team
Purchasing Team
Graduate School of Public Health
College of Medicine
Graduate School of Clinical Dentistry
College of Health Science
Health Sciences Library
Office of Industry & Academy Cooperation, College of Medicine
Office of Health Industriy & Academy Cooperation
University Part
HOSPITAL(Anam, Guro, Ansan)
Hospital Part
Office of Planning
Office of Clinical Affairs
Office of Management & Administration

## 4. 병원 조직도의 예 2

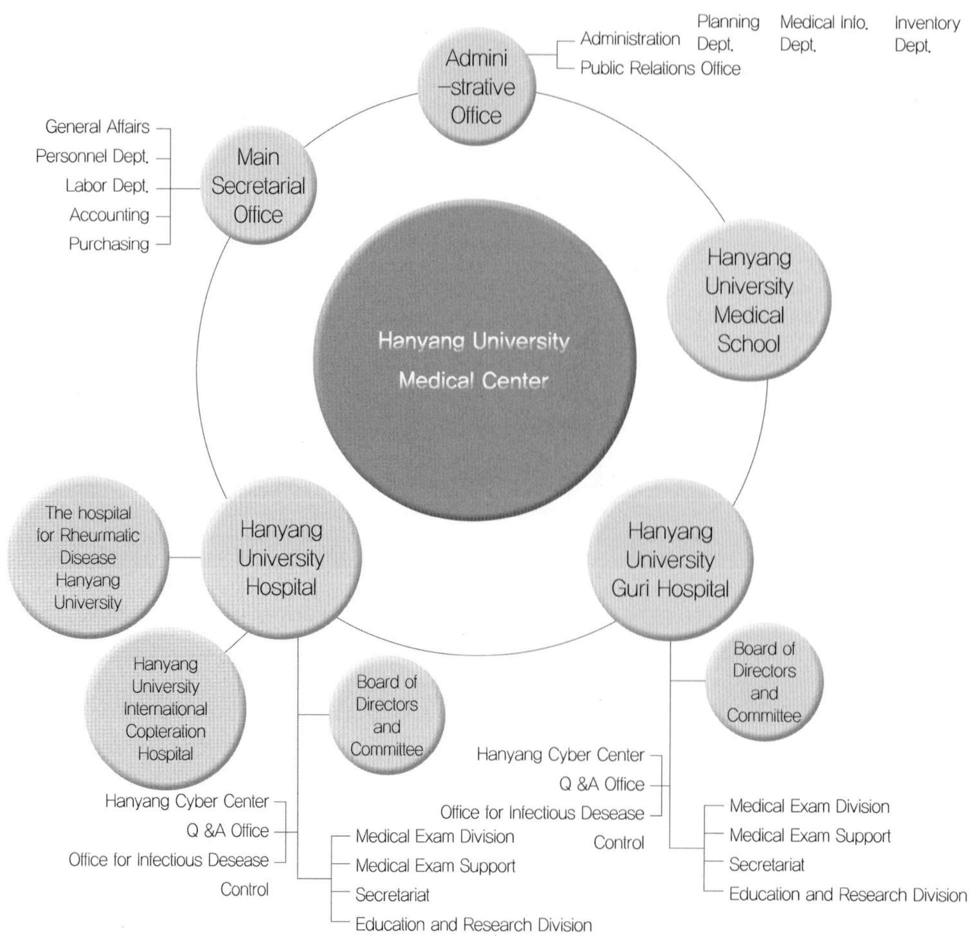
Hanyang University Medical Center
Admini-strative Office
Administration
Planning Dept.
Medical Info. Dept.
Inventory Dept.
Public Relations Office
Main Secretarial Office
General Affairs
Personnel Dept.
Labor Dept.
Accounting
Purchasing
Hanyang University Medical School
Hanyang University Hospital
The hospital for Rheurmatic Disease Hanyang University
Hanyang University International Copteration Hospital
Board of Directors and Committee
Hanyang Cyber Center
Q &A Office
Office for Infectious Desease Control
Medical Exam Division
Medical Exam Support
Secretariat
Education and Research Division
Hanyang University Guri Hospital
Board of Directors and Committee
Hanyang Cyber Center
Q &A Office
Office for Infectious Desease Control
Medical Exam Division
Medical Exam Support
Secretariat
Education and Research Division

## 5. 국회 조직도

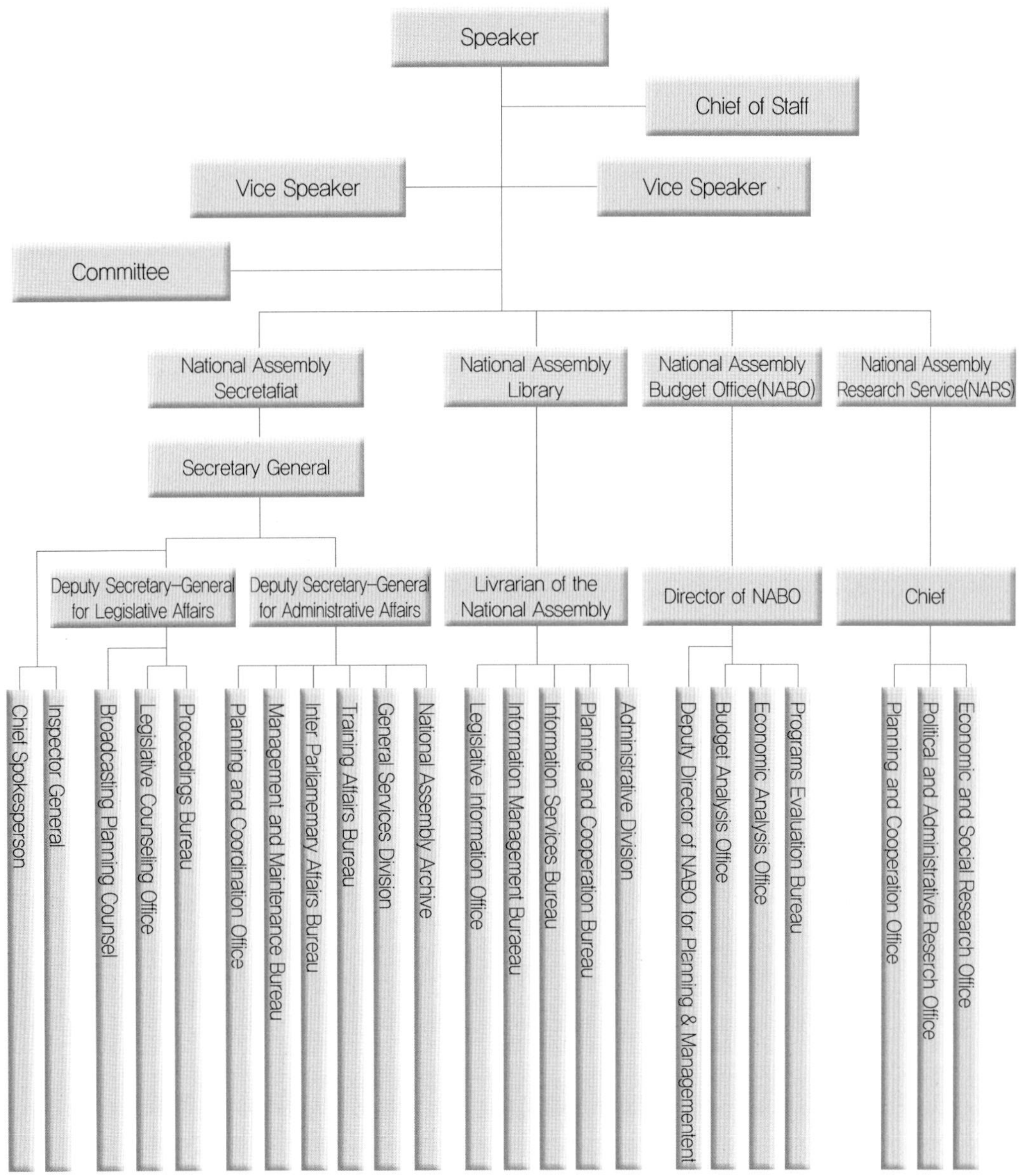
Speaker
Chief of Staff
Vice Speaker
Vice Speaker
Committee
National Assembly Secretafiat
National Assembly Library
National Assembly Budget Office(NABO)
National Assembly Research Service(NARS)
Secretary General
Deputy Secretary-General for Legislative Affairs
Deputy Secretary-General for Administrative Affairs
Livrarian of the National Assembly
Director of NABO
Chief
Chief Spokesperson
Inspector General
Broadcasting Planning Counsel
Legislative Counseling Office
Proceedings Bureau
Planning and Coordination Office
Management and Maintenance Bureau
Inter Parliamentary Affairs Bureau
Training Affairs Bureau
General Services Division
National Assembly Archive
Legislative Information Office
Information Management Bureaau
Information Services Bureau
Planning and Cooperation Bureau
Administrative Division
Deputy Director of NABO for Planning & Managemenent
Budget Analysis Office
Economic Analysis Office
Programs Evaluation Bureau
Planning and Cooperation Office
Political and Administrative Reserch Office
Economic and Social Research Office

## 6. 정부기관 조직도의 예 1

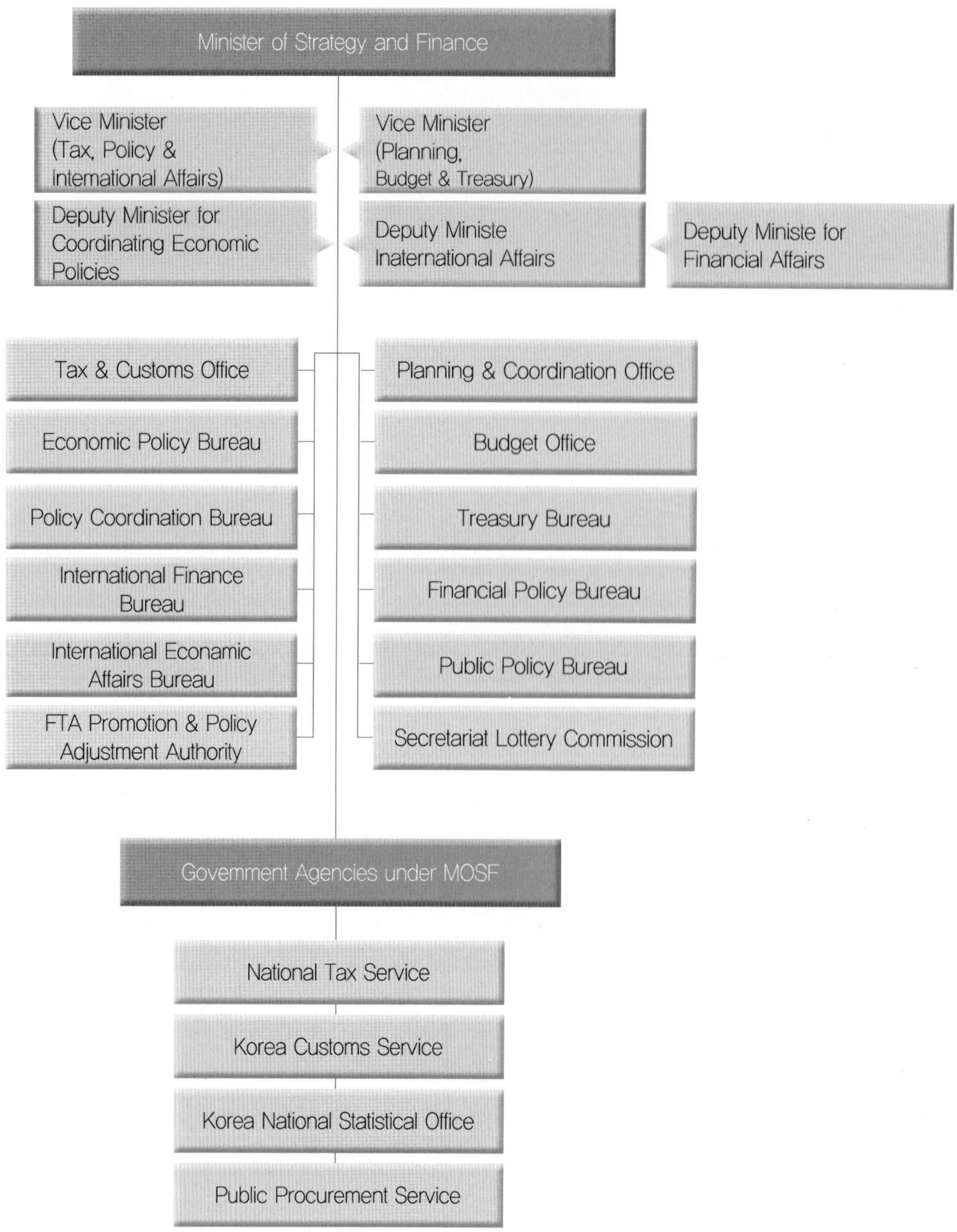

## 7. 정부기관 조직도의 예 2

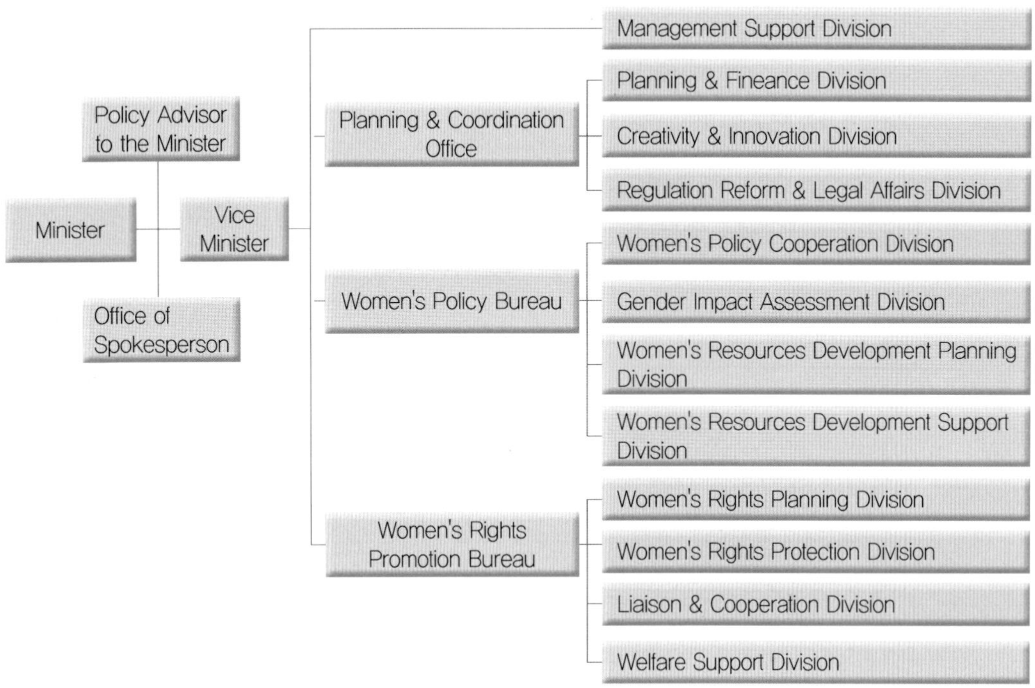

## 예제 1

다음 그래프를 올바르게 묘사하도록 문장의 밑줄을 채우시오

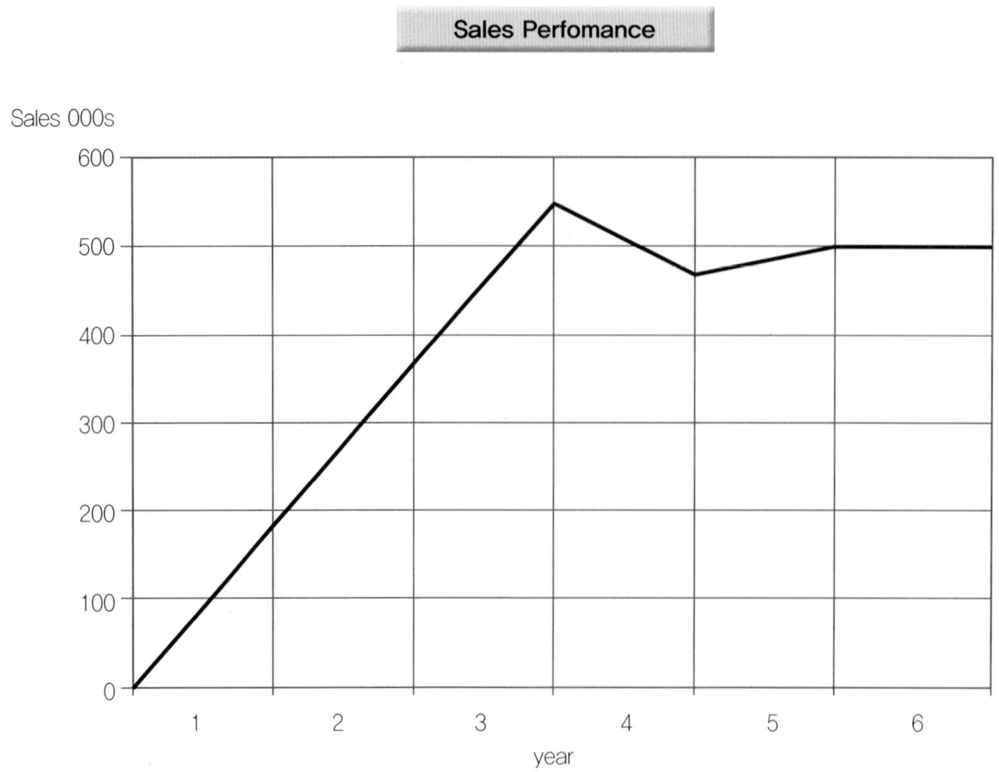


**1**. In the first three years, sales ___________ steadily.

**2**. The following year sales ___________ badly.

**3**. Then in year five they ___________ again.

**4**. They ___________ at this figure in year six.

## 예제 2

다음의 기업전략에 관한 Conditions(조건)과 Results(결과)를 보기와 같이 알맞게 연결한 후, If로 연결된 문장을 작성하시오.

| Conditions | Results |
|---|---|
| 1. Reduce prices | a. Cut unit costs |
| 2. Margins smaller | b. Job losses |
| 3. Increase production | c. Reduced sales |
| 4. Invest in new plant | d. Market share increases |
| 5. Upgrade product | e. Cut profits |
| 6. Higher prices | f. Unit costs come down |
| 7. Reduce manufacturing costs | g. Higher profits |
| 8. Sub-contract production | h. Adapt to market |

________________________________________.

________________________________________.

________________________________________.

________________________________________.

________________________________________.

________________________________________.

________________________________________.

________________________________________.

## 예제 3

다음의 consumer survey에 관한 질문지를 읽고 조사자가 해야 할 알맞은 질문들의 밑줄을 채우시오.

# Ace Market Research

## Consumer Survey

① Name ______________________________

② Address ______________________________

③ Telephone ______________________________

④ Accommodation    Own home ☐    Rent ☐
Hotel ☐    Other ...... ☐

⑤ Place of work : Husband ______________________________
Wife ______________________________

⑥ Place of study : Child 1 ______________________________
Child 2 ______________________________

⑦ Money spent on last summer holiday ______________________________

⑧ Location of last vacation ______________________________

① __________ is your name?

② __________ do you live?

③ __________ is your telephone number?

④ __________ you live in your own house?

⑤ __________ do you and your wife work?

⑥ __________ school does your child go to?

⑦ __________ __________ did you spend on last summer holiday?

⑧ __________ was your last vacation?

## 3. Agendas & Minutes(의제 및 회의록)

### 1. Meeting Agendas(회의 일정표, 회의 안건)

Agenda는 회의에서 다루어질 안건들이 무엇인지 미리 보기 위하여 반드시 회의 전에 제공되어야 한다. 회의 전에 회의안을 주의 깊게 살펴보고 언제 어디에서 회의가 열리는지 등의 정보를 정확이 알고 있어야 하며, 미리 본인의 몫을 충분히 준비하여 회의 진행 중에 닥칠지 모르는 질문에 대비 할 수 있도록 한다.

Sample Agenda

**SALES & MARKETING MONTHLY MEETING**

*Date:* 3 April *Time:* 10.30 *Venue:* Meeting room 6

*Called by:* Sara Filfil (Sales & Marketing Director and Chair)

*Attendees:* All Sales Representatives: Hannah Pepper, Jack Stone, Adam Lamb, Tanya Prakash, Khem Singh.

*Recording secretary:* Rory Morgan.

*Please read:* March sales report attached. *Please bring:* n/a

**AGENDA**

1 Apologies
2 Approval of minutes of last meeting
3 Matters arising
4 Sales results for March
5 New incentives and rewards
6 AOB

위의 회의 일정표를 읽고 미리 준비해야 할 사항을 모두 고르시오.

1. Read the minutes from the last meeting, so that I will be in a position to approve them. ( )
2. Remind myself about the company's health and safety policies. ( )
3. Read the March sales report. ( )
4. Read the July sales report. ( )
5. Revise my sales targets. ( )
6. Think about any points to raise during AOB. ( )

## 2. Minutes of the meeting(회의록)

반면, 회의록은 회의가 끝난 후에 배포된다. 회의 중 각 안건에 대하여 어떠한 논의가 진행이 되었는지 그 내용과 합의 사항, 그리고 구체적인 행동 계획안(action points) 등을 문서로 기록한 것이다. 회의록을 받은 후에는 전체적으로 훑어 읽으면서 자신과 관련된 부분은 구체적이며 꼼꼼하게 읽어야 한다. 자신이 한 발언이 정확하게 기록되었는지, 빠지거나 더해진 부분은 없는지, 자신에게 맡겨진 action points가 무엇인지 등을 체크해야 한다. 따라서 Action points는 그 다음 회의에 승인되어야 할 것이다.

회의록을 작성하는 사람은 회의가 진행되는 동안 회의 참가자들의 발언과 누가 어떤 task를 담당하게 되는지 등의 중요한 사항을 빠짐없이 메모해 두었다가 회의 직후에 문서로 작성하도록 한다. 회의록의 형식은 정해진 것이 없고 기관마다 다르지만, 기본적으로 다음의 사항을 포함한다.

1. the name of the organization;
2. the place, date, and time of the meeting;
3. whether the meeting is regular (monthly, special, and so on);
4. the name of the person presiding;
5. a record of attendance (for small meetings, a list of those present or absent; for large meetings, the number of members in attendance);
6. a reference to the minutes of the pervious meeting (a statement that they were read and either accepted or revised, or that the reading was dispensed with);
7. an account of all reports, motions, or resolutions made (including all necessary details and the results o votes taken);
8. the date, time, and place of the next meeting;
9. the time of adjournment.

## Sample Minutes

### MINUTES OF SALES & MARKETING MONTHLY MEETING

The monthly Sales & Marketing meeting of Philips Pharmaceutical Sales was held at 10.30 on 3 April at offices of company.

*Attendees*

Sara Filfil (Chair), Hannah Pepper, Adam Lamb, Tanya Prakash, Khem Singh, Rory Morgan

*Apologies*

Jack Stone sent apologies because unwell.

*Approval of Minutes*

Rory Morgan presented minutes of Sales & Marketing Monthly meeting, 4 March for approval. Unanimously approved as presented.

*Matters arising*

- Adam Lamb noted that order not yet placed for new SJE12 sales software, approved at last meeting.
- Sara Filfil to purchase before next meeting.

*Sales results for March*

Sara Filfil drew attention to March sales report:

- Sara Filfil noted that sales were down by 2.4% on previous month.
- Adam Lamb suggested possible cause was special promotion run by Mastersons Pharmaceuticals. Adam Lamb to research upcoming promotions by major competitors for presentation at next meeting.
- Sara Filfil noted that despite drop in sales all employees met individual sales targets. Special commendation given to Hannah Pepper who exceeded target by 8%.

*New incentives and rewards*

Sara Filfil announced two new initiatives and rewards:

- If a Sales Representative exceeds sales targets by more than 15%, they will receive increased commission of 7.5% of total revenue on all subsequent sales.
- In December, a five-star holiday for a family of four will be awarded to Sales Representative with highest quantity of sales during year.

*AOB*

- Tanya Prakash to circulate sample version of new quarterly newsletter by 15 April.
- All attendees to provide feedback on newsletter to Tanya Prakash by end of month.
- Hannah Pepper to coordinate collection for HR Director's maternity present by 8 April.

위의 회의록을 읽고 다음 물음에 답하시오.

1. 이 회사의 Sales & Marketing에 관한 회의는 몇 시에 어디에서 열렸습니까?

______________________________

2. 이 회의의 의장은 누구이며 회의록은 누가 기록하였습니까?

______________________________

3. Adam Lamb은 지난 회의로부터 어떠한 활동 계획(action point)에 관심을 가졌나요?

______________________________

4. 3월 판매량은 지난달에 비하여 올라갔나요? 내려갔나요?

______________________________

5. 이번 달 판매 목표치에 도달하지 못한 사람은 누구인가요?

______________________________

6. 특별 수상에 발탁된 판매자 대표는 누구인가요?

______________________________

## 저자 약력

**홍순이**(洪淳伊) / Soon Yee Hong

이화여자대학교 법정대학 비서학과 졸업

경영학 석사(재무관리전공) - 한양대학교

경영학 박사(인사 · 조직전공) - 이화여자대학교

(주) 유공, Credit Agricole Indosuez, Lehman Brothers Inc. 근무

한양여자대학교 영어과 강사역임

대림대학교 국제사무행정과 교수 역임(1995-2015)

University of Illinois at Chicago Visiting Scholar

한국비서학회 회장 역임(2007-2009)

**현)** 커리어 · 커뮤니케이션 연구소 대표

대전대학교 일반대학원 융합컨설팅학과 대우교수

전북대학교 산학협력단 겸임교수

NCS 및 신직업자격 보완위원

◆ **주요연구**

"비서의 재교육에 관한 연구"(1995), "전문분야별 비서의 역할 및 업무에 관한 연구"(1996), "한.일 비서교육 수료자의 비교연구"(한일 국제공동연구)(1997), 세기 대림대학의 비젼실현을 위한 비서행정과 기여도 제고방안"(1999), 원격근무와 조직효과성 관계에 있어서 상사신뢰와 공정성 지각의 조절효과에 관한 연구(2003), The Effect of Teleworking and Its Moderators in Korea(2004) 외 다수

◆ **저서**

비서학개론, 비서실무실습, 비즈니스 커뮤니케이션 실무론, 비서실무 Workbook, 현장중심의 비서실무 Case Study Practical Business Writing, Business English Conversation 등 다수

**윤혜정**(尹惠楨) / Hae Jung Yun

이화여자대학교 상경대학 비서학과 졸업(경영학 부전공)

연세대학교 경영대학원 졸업(경영학 석사)

연세대학교 정보대학원 졸업(정보시스템 박사)

건국대-University of Illinois Joint TESOL 과정 수료

TOEIC 990점(만점) 취득

주)케이씨텍, 다큐멘텀코리아, 화광교역(주) 근무

대림대학교 국제사무행정과 겸임교수

연세대학교 언더우드국제대학, 이화여자대학교 국제사무학과 강사

American University 박사후연구원, 연세대학교 BK사업단 연구교수

**현)** 이화여자대학교 국제사무학과 조교수

◆ **주요연구**

"An Examination of Work Exhaustion in the Mobile Enterprise Environment", Technological Forecasting & Social Change, Vol. 100 (2015), "A New Open Door: The Smartphone's Impact on Work-to-Life Conflict, Stress, and Resistance", International Journal of Electronic Commerce, Vol. 16, No. 4 (2012) 외 다수

NCS 기반

# Business Correspdence II (활용편)

초판 1쇄 발행 2009년 2월 10일
2 판 2쇄 발행 2019년 8월 25일

**저 자** 홍순이 · 윤혜정

**펴 낸 이** 임 순 재
**펴 낸 곳** **한올출판사**
**등 록** 제11-403호
**주 소** 서울시 마포구 모래내로 83(성산동, 한올빌딩 3층)
**전 화** (02)376-4298(대표)
**팩 스** (02)302-8073
**홈페이지** www.hanol.co.kr
**e-메 일** hanol@hanol.co.kr

ISBN 979-11-5685-415-9